THRIVE

DON'T JUST SURVIVE

A MILLENNIAL MOM'S GUIDE TO FINANCIAL FREEDOM

CHERISH WINSOR

THE MILLENNIAL mom

This publication is for informational purposes only. It is sold with the understanding that neither the author nor the publisher is engaged in rendering legal, investment, accounting, or other professional services.

Nothing contained in this publication constitutes a solicitation, recommendation, endorsement, or offer by the publisher or author to buy or sell any securities or other financial instruments in any jurisdiction in which such solicitation or offer would be unlawful under the securities laws of such jurisdiction.

While the publisher and author have used their best efforts in preparing this book, they make no representations or warranties with respect to the accuracy or completeness of the contents of this book and specifically disclaim any implied warranties of merchantability or fitness for a particular purpose. The publisher and the author are providing this book and its contents on an "as is" basis. The advice and strategies contained herein may not be suitable for your situation. You should not rely on any revenue, sales, or earnings information provided in this book as any kind of promise, guarantee, or expectation of any level of success or earnings. You should consult with a professional when appropriate. Neither the publisher nor the author shall be liable for any loss of profit or any other commercial damages, including but not limited to special, incidental, consequential, personal, or other damages.

Cover design by Diren Yardimli
Internal design by HMDPUBLISHING

The Millennial Mom Ltd.

www.themillennialmom.ca

Special discounts are available on quantity purchases. Contact the publisher for more information.

ISBN: 978-1-7383914-0-0

FREE GIFTS FOR YOU

Because you're awesome and I want you to succeed, I've included these free gifts to help you on your journey to becoming financially free:

THRIVE WORKBOOK

A perfect companion to accompany your journey through this book. The Thrive workbook includes helpful exercises to help you chart your path to a financially free future.

THRIVE AUDIOBOOK

Listen along in the carpool lane, Starbucks drive-thru, or on your way to work.

Visit my website to claim your free gifts today!
www.cherishwinsor.com/freebies

EARLY PRAISE FOR THRIVE:

"Clear, relatable and shockingly enjoyable to read."

KATE BOTHNER, author of *And So I Roam* and *Fever Dreams and Ill-Begotten Things*

Thrive is an essential book for any Canadian millennial who is interested in financial freedom. With accuracy and expertise, Cherish takes readers through her story in a way that will leave them inspired."

SHELLY ZEV, Editor at www.shellyzev.com

"This book has the power to carry female millennials into a financially balanced and secure future."

TORI LEWIS

"Intuitive to the challenges of our economic climate with personal anecdotes to make finance a topic that is enjoyable to learn while addressing the mental implications of money woes and fears. A most enjoyable read!"

KARLI WESSLERBANKS

"This book is going to enrich the lives of millennials."

STEPHANIE GREEN

CONTENTS

INTRODUCTION

I want to begin this book by posing a question to you, the reader. If you woke up tomorrow debt-free, with an income that allowed you to choose how you spent your time, what would you do?

Throughout the pages of this book, I'll share with you my journey of how I went from a homeless and pregnant mom of three to a successful corporate leader, business owner and real estate investor. I'll also share the tips and tricks I learned along the way so that I could leave the corporate world behind and focus instead on my family and the things that make me happy. Retiring before forty isn't the norm, especially for Millennials or people who have struggled financially, like I did.

We're more than just our bank account and as you will read in this book; the way we look at money and finances affects so many aspects of our lives and personalities. While much of your financial outlook is personal, there have been several world events, social or cultural shifts and life-stage disruptions that have affected the Millennial generation at a critical time in our lives. The world we grew up in – from innovations in technology to recessions (four since the early 80s) have shaped who we are and, more importantly, our relationship with money.

At the time of writing this book, it is early 2024 which means that Millennials are between the ages of 28 – 43 (born in 1981 – 1996) and are mostly in our thirties. According to Statistics Canada, before the end of this decade, Millennials are expected to outnumber baby boomers and we already make up the largest percentage of the working population at 33%.[1] Anecdotally, we're fulfilled less by work, and we find it less rewarding than previous generations.

Millennials are working, raising kids, paying off debt and still have student loans. Retirement, saving, inflation and other adult things are on our minds. We're at the age where we are real grown-ups with real grown-up issues. Because many of us are smack-dab in our child-rearing years, our child-care costs rival our mortgage or rent payments.

In Canada, we're facing an unprecedented housing crisis. It has squeezed many people, not just Millennials, out of the housing market with depleting supply and high interest rates. For those of us who rent, our housing costs are higher than previous generations, even while adjusting for our decent incomes.

We have little job security, despite being more highly educated than past generations.[2] We value work-life balance, flexibility and we don't buy into the job loyalty of previous generations – likely because we've lost access to indexed pension plans, 40-hour work weeks and respect from employers. We're more likely to switch jobs (quiet quitting, anyone?) when they don't suit us but we're also more likely to have to settle for term contracts rather than indeterminate positions.

On average, we owe nearly fifty thousand dollars in unsecured debt, mostly in credit cards. A third of us are carrying student loan debt[3] and forty percent of us have mortgages.[4]

Our parents are aging and hitting retirement age. Of those who have yet to retire, some will be able to by the time they are 65, while many others have little savings and will rely on federal benefits and their Canada Pension Plan payouts. Many of our parents missed out on the pension plans of their older boomer counterparts and are expected to self-fund their retirement. Because of this, the old ways of thinking about retirement no longer apply. For us, and for many of our parents, we're just making it up as we go.

Thanks to the pandemic, better technology, and our less-than-stellar social skills, more of us work from home than ever before. Also, thanks to the pandemic, many of us, albeit along with other generations, have moved away from the larger cities in hopes of a better work-life balance. Prior to 2020, more than a third of the populations of large Canadian urban centers were Millennials. I'd bet that number will reduce in the coming years.

Altogether, we've had a bleak first few decades and we're up against a lot. A tough job market, wage stagnation, globalization, and the pandemic have resulted in delayed wealth-generation opportunities. The news isn't all bad though. The silver lining, as we all heard many times growing up, is that what doesn't kill you will make you stronger. Hopefully.

We're more than our Starbucks lattes, yoga pants and avocado toast. As a generation, we know how to make bank. In 2016, Canadian Millennials were making 30 percent more than Gen Xers or Boomers when they were the same age, even when adjusting for inflation. What's more, by 2022, Millennials were making about 75 percent of the average Canadian wage, despite being early in our careers.[5]

The gig economy has taught us to be resourceful with many of us having multiple income streams. Higher housing costs have taught us that less can be more, which is probably why minimalism is so on trend. Watching our parents and older friends or colleagues struggle with retirement planning has made us realise that we need to take this seriously. We just don't know how.

Taken together, our earning ability, debt load and savings (even if not for retirement), have us Millennials seemingly sitting pretty. Our net worth is over 1.5 times what Gen Xers were able to achieve at the same age.[6] This tells me that we are comfortable with debt and still have the ability to earn the income required for a financially free future. We just need to shift our mindset and learn a little more about personal finance so that we get more out of the money we do have.

You may be asking, how do we as Millennial moms, Millennial women, make the most of our money, set our kids up for success, and plan for retirement, all while living our best life? That's what I'm going to show you in this book. As you've read, the building blocks are there, we just need to rearrange things a little and shift our mindset.

My youngest brother was born in 1991, eight years after I was, and I feel like we grew up very differently from each other. On the other hand, I have two Gen X siblings that I can relate to and who have had similar financial experiences. With fifteen years between the oldest and youngest of us Millennials, we're still a varied generation and some of this may apply to you while other parts of it will not. Generally speaking, though, this is what it means to be a Canadian Millennial in 2024.

Most books about finances are typically written by authors who have expertise in the financial industry or by authors who have successfully navigated financial challenges. I fall into the latter camp, and throughout my journey towards financial freedom, I have learned first-hand and developed my own strategies for budgeting, saving, investing, managing debt, and entrepreneurship, all so that I can spend my time as I want.

Think of me as a girlfriend sharing bits and pieces of my life, the ups and downs, the struggles, and successes. I'm here to

encourage you and share in your journey by sharing my own. Rather than reading my life story, you'll find bits of my journey all throughout the coming chapters.

While I've experienced homelessness and started my financial journey from a place that is likely different than yours, this book isn't just for women who are struggling financially. I believe that every Millennial mom can improve their financial well-being and benefit from more financial knowledge. If you're living paycheque-to-paycheque and feeling overwhelmed with debt and bills, you might find relevance in my story and learn, as I did, to shift your mindset (discussed in chapter five) and take hold of your finances. Or, if you've followed a more traditional path and are living a comfortable lifestyle, you'll likely find useful information to make your money grow through my strategies for wealth generation, discussed in chapters six and seven.

You've picked this book up for a reason and I hope that you find what you are looking for in its pages. If not, my website www.cherishwinsor.com is filled with additional nuggets of knowledge, resources, and recommended reading. I reference it often but don't feel any pressure to visit. This is your journey and I'm here to help you.

For years, I hated that I was a Millennial. Having been born in the early Eighties, I felt that I fit in more with Gen X than the stereotypical Millennials. At the time, we had a bad rap and were seen as the lazy, entitled, participation-trophy generation. The word Millennial became synonymous with a twenty-something who didn't have their life together yet.

As time went on, and as we all aged, I think we became a little more vocal – something we aren't usually very good at. We stood up for ourselves and started to point out that many of us were nearing our forties. We have careers and children, mortgages, and credit card bills. As a generation, we had grown up and the world started to notice.

Now, technically I am an elder Millennial or Xennial which explains why I have such a strong tie to the generation before us. As an elder Millennial (sounds wise, doesn't it?), I want to share what I've learned with the rest of my generation, so that we can all prosper and have financially free futures.

Less than a year ago, at age thirty-nine, I retired from my career as a corporate relations executive at a northern Canadian mine. My partner and I had started the process of working towards an early retirement a few years ago and our initial plans saw us working for another two years. We worked for the same company and planned our end-date around a natural point in the mining cycle, rather than our personal financial situation. Due to company restructuring, we were both able to leave our jobs years earlier than expected and because of our earlier planning, we had enough passive income and investments to allow us to retire.

In that line of work, I would start each day by scanning headlines and emails and reviewing what might have happened since the night before. I worked for an international company that had people working around the clock so a lot could happen overnight. It's also my nature to want to be "in the know", which meant I wanted to be prepared both for what was going on at work and in the community.

Things are a little different now. I do still check emails, review the headlines and spend some time reading social media, but that's pretty much where the similarities end. If I'm disciplined, I'll scroll right past those Reels but more than likely, I'll watch a few and then wonder where the time went. It's something I'm working on.

I might start my day with a coffee and a plan. I often do this in my pajamas. If it's summer, I'm on my deck in the sunshine.

It may be 7 am or it may be 10 am – it all depends on the day and what is going on with my family. I no longer have a set schedule to follow. My days are my own and how I structure them is up to me. I still have responsibilities, of course. I am a mom of six with multiple businesses, after all. But that's the true magic of financial freedom; I don't have to be tied to my desk all day, every day. I can enjoy my family and be there when they need me.

What's the difference between retirement and work, you may ask? Well, it's that I have financial freedom without the stress of deadlines or meetings for a big company that ultimately, does not care about me. Time is now my friend rather than something there just isn't enough of. I no longer live my life by the clock or spend long days at my computer, barely seeing the sun or stretching my legs. I'm not exhausted by dinner time with no energy left for my family. When my uncle was sick, I could hop on a plane and be there when he needed me.

For me, having an open schedule was one of the most important reasons to become financially free. Corporate jobs are not for the weak, especially as you move up through the ranks. They are also a huge time suck. When my daughter was eight, she did a series of impressions featuring her family members. Her portrayal of me was a busy workaholic who didn't have time to look up from her computer. That hit me right in the feels. As a parent, it was a moment that I'll never forget. I realised that being present for my kids was more important than whatever I was working on at my day job. I just needed to figure out how to bring home the bacon AND get to hang with my kids. Simple, right?

What I've learned over the years is that it can be simple, but it depends on your goals and personal situation too. When you know what it is you want out of life, or even just for this stage, you can put together a plan to achieve it. Without a destination, you're likely to waste a lot of time and money going in directions that don't help you get there. You also need a reason, something that is personal to you and that will encourage and replenish you through the difficulties you may face on your way to your destination. I call this your Why and will share more details in the next chapter.

Being a mom is tough; most days are just keeping up with the demands of life, which can be exhausting. Life should be more than just an endless to-do list. That's where I come in. I'll walk you through the basics of money management and show you how I achieved financial freedom. I don't want this to be another burden that you need to add to your days. Instead, this book is meant to be encouraging and informative. My hope is that each time you pick it up, whether in the carpool lane or after the kids have been tucked into bed, you close it feeling encouraged to move forward on your path to financial freedom.

I wrote this book to encourage and support moms just like me, who are feeling overwhelmed with things that need doing but underwhelmed with life and want more. I feel privileged that you've chosen to take the time to read through these pages and spend your precious time with me.

There will likely be pages or chapters that hold little relevance to you and it's ok to skip those. I read personal finance books often and try to read chapters I think I've already mastered because sometimes there are hidden nuggets of wisdom. I've included Too Long, Didn't Read (TLDR) headings for each chapter so that you know in advance what will be covered. I encourage you to have a quick read even if the chapter doesn't seem to apply to you or your situation. I mean, you never know when you will stumble upon some truth and that TLDR may just turn into a Too Long, Definitely Read.

So, grab a coffee, tea, or glass of pinot and find a cozy spot while we start you on your journey to financial freedom.

Ready? Let's go.

SECTION

One

BELIEVE IN YOURSELF

CHAPTER 1
YOUR WHY

TLDR: Before you can start working towards financial freedom, you need to know where you're going. What is it that will motivate you and keep you moving towards that goal?

Before you jump in the car and turn out of your driveway, you need to know where you're going. The same is true for your personal finance journey. Before you can start working towards financial freedom, you need to know where you're going, the path to get to your destination, and, of course, how to drive. In this chapter, we will talk about the first part: where you're going. In other words, what you want to work towards, which for many of us is financial freedom. Ask yourself, what is it that you want to achieve by reading this book and implementing the strategies and exercises?

I've struggled to choose a point in my life that I'd consider the beginning of my journey to financial freedom. Like everyone, I've had ups and downs, starts, and stops, good years and bad years. I started working when I was 15 and had quit school so I could work full-time at 16. I rented a room from a sketchy older guy and did little other than work. I didn't make much and was always broke, but I also didn't know any better. Living paycheque to paycheque was the norm I grew up with.

Pregnant at 17, I continued to work fast food jobs, but I mostly relied on a local church's donation bin for all the baby clothes and items I needed. I had no long-term plan to support myself or my child; by the time he was born, I was broke, I couldn't afford childcare and I was living with my parents. Something had to change and thankfully, I realised education was the best path forward. I completed my GED, enrolled in a college graphic design program, and moved to a new city. Going to school, raising young kids, and struggling to pay my bills became my norm for the next seven years.

I graduated from university at twenty-five with a degree in sociology, three kids in tow and pregnant with my fourth. A few weeks later, we were kicked out of our rented home because the power had been disconnected when I failed to keep up with the bill. My rent was paid for the month but without power, my landlord was able to evict me without notice. By the time I picked my oldest son up from school that day, he no longer had a home to come back to.

We couch-surfed with whoever would take us in and spent some time in shelters. My fourth son was born during this time. I'll never forget the moment I was asked to fill out the hospital forms and had no address to write down. It was the lowest point in my life, and I guess that is where my journey to financial freedom really began: at rock bottom.

My poor money management had caught up to me. Throughout my college and university years, I supported myself and my kids with student loans and supplemented with subsidies for childcare and rent. I knew I'd have to pay it all back eventually, but I reasoned that I would have a better job and would be able to afford the payments. This mindset allowed me to get my education, which was a necessity for my future success, but it also set me up for years of financial struggle.

Things were always tight, but I was able to keep everything going so long as that student loan cheque showed up every four months. When I graduated, it was the first time in seventeen semesters that I didn't have that student loan come in. Instead, I tried to get by on income support from the government, which was less than a thousand dollars a month for a family of five.

I remember a conversation with one of my children around that time. Always the bleeding heart, my son was telling me something about a group of people he considered poor. It was obvious in the way he was speaking that he didn't consider himself in that group. I couldn't even pay attention to the rest of what he was saying because I was so focused on the fact that he didn't know. We were poor and yet he hadn't realised it. I was somehow proud of keeping him from feeling the effects of poverty and ashamed for not being able to give him more. That was fifteen years ago, and I've worked every single day to make sure that rock bottom wasn't the end of my story or my kids'.

As a testament to how far we've come, my fourth son, the one who was born homeless, has traveled extensively, for both pleasure and as part of his high-performance soccer team. Last year, he visited seven countries over a three-month period. He's flown business class to play in a weekend soccer tournament. His siblings have all had similar experiences and it's only because I made an intentional choice to do better for them and I've worked hard to achieve it. Giving them those experiences was my Why, my reason for putting in the work to get us here.

You have likely never experienced homelessness but that doesn't mean your journey has been any less tough. You are reading this book because you desire more from life, in whatever form that takes. Your Why is what will keep you motivated when things get hard. It will encourage you when thinking about your future. It will replenish you when you need a little pick-me-up.

Let's spend a little bit of time pondering and dreaming about what that could look like for you.

To start, grab your inspirational notebook, the notes app on your phone, or use the online version from my website www.Cherishwinsor.com. What I want you to do is jot down whatever comes to your mind as you work through this exercise.

Exercise 1: Finding Your Why

Before you write down anything, start by thinking about the question I posed at the beginning of this book: If money wasn't an issue, what would you be doing right now? Give yourself a little time to dream about what that might look like.

You can just free-flow your thoughts, writing down whatever comes to mind, even if it seems silly or far-fetched. If you need a little inspiration, here are some things to get you thinking:

- If you didn't have to go to work today, would you still go?
- Would you have a different job that you enjoyed more?
- Would you volunteer at a charity or your kids' school?
- Would you spend your days with your kids or finally get around to those projects you've been putting off?
- Could you spend more time on your hobbies or take up a new one?

For the next part, I want you to consider how it would feel to spend your day doing the things you've outlined. Visualize yourself living that life and put yourself into a moment. How does it feel? Write that down.

Finally, you're going to pull everything you've written so far into one or two sentences. Using one of the fill-in-the-blank sentences below, try to capture your Why. If you're more comfortable using your own language, that's okay too.

I want to be financially free so that I can spend my time ___
____
____
and experience/feel ______________________________.

My future looks bright. By taking control of my finances, I will feel ______________________ and be able to spend my time ______________________________________.

Okay, pencils down. That wasn't so bad, was it? Or maybe it was but I promise it is important. Unless you've got a stellar sense of direction, you can't get to your destination if you don't know where it is or how to get there. Only you can draw the road map that works for you, but this exercise and the others in this book will help you create your path.

If you're still stuck with what to write, here are some real-life examples from others who have been right where you are:

> **I want to be financially free so I can spend my time doing the things I enjoy and feel unburdened and less anxious.**
>
> **I want to be financially free so I can provide my children with opportunities for their future and present parents who are engaged with them, free of the distractions caused by financial stress and overburdening careers.**
>
> **I want to be financially free so that I can spend my time travelling, running my business the way I want to, and feeling relaxed and fulfilled.**
>
> **My future is bright. By taking control of my finances, I will feel energized and relaxed and be able to spend my time how I want, with the people that matter to me.**

Now that you've spent a little time dreaming and have a better sense of how being financially free could change your life, we're going to explore your personal relationship with money and some of the ways you've been influenced to think about it. Then, in Section Two, we'll spend some time learning about financial basics and start to build your path to that exciting new future you've been dreaming about.

CHAPTER 2
START AT THE BEGINNING

TLDR: Many of us know less about money than we'd like. Our knowledge and our viewpoint have been shaped by our upbringing and the people we've surrounded ourselves with. Whatever your relationship with money, you can change it and build true generational wealth.

We all have a personal relationship with money that we've developed from our past experiences with it. How you grew up, the kinds of jobs you've had, the friends and conversations you've had, and how money was talked about (or not), all contribute to how you now relate to money.

While reading this chapter, your task is to consider how your relationship with money and finance was formed and how it developed throughout the stages of your life. Armed with this information, you'll be able to restructure how you look at money and learn to use it properly.

You may have come from a home where money was never discussed or where you saw your parents struggle to pay bills. You may have been told you couldn't have something because your parents couldn't afford it. You may have received an allowance, or not. You may have heard your parents discuss their investments or been taught specifically about financial concepts. For most of us, especially Millennial women raised by Boomer parents, we likely know less than we'd like, which is probably why you're reading this book.

I've often heard the complaint that our schools do not teach young people the practical side of life; how to do taxes (or what taxes even are), how to budget or make a financial plan, and maybe most importantly, how to save for retirement. These are all important lessons that young people should be taught. While I agree with the sentiment that we need to learn these concepts at a young age, I don't necessarily agree that school is the best place for kids to learn them.

Parents are in the best position to show kids how money works in a practical way. They are living it every day whether through their own budgets, bills, or investments. Of course, there's a place for schools to support and reinforce good money management but it's through our everyday viewing of those around us, including our parents, where we learn our fundamental skills.

I grew up in a large family. Having five siblings certainly isn't the norm for most Millennials but that's where I found myself. My parents always owned their home and kept food on the table, but I always thought of us on the poorer end of the spectrum. I didn't think we were "poor," but I knew we didn't have much money to go around.

When my cousins went to Disneyland, I knew there wasn't any point in asking my parents to go. It was just understood that we were not that kind of family. Trips like that were for *other* people. I have a friend who had a similar childhood and even as a working adult who could afford to join his best friend on an annual beach holiday, he still believed he wasn't part of the crowd that did things like that.

These kinds of experiences taught me that money was scarce and as a kid without the means to change my place in the world, money seemed elusive. It wasn't something I could attain but it was something I wanted because it meant I could do the fun things that other people in my life could.

As humans, we love to categorize things. It's ingrained in all of us, and allows us to navigate social and cultural complexities, helping us to better understand peoples' thoughts, beliefs, actions, and interactions. By automatically categorizing things, we are better able to understand and move through this world quickly and efficiently. We know that foods from the fruits or vegetables categories are better for us than foods that belong to the salty snacks category. Instead of having to consider the nutritional value of each item, we categorize it automatically to free up our brains for other things. This is the same reason why many of us will continue to vote for a single political party, regardless of who the leader is or how their politics align with our own. We like to put people and things in groups to easily understand them.

When it comes to your financial upbringing, you have likely categorized yourself into a class or group of people you see yourself belonging to. Having done this, usually at a young age, it is tough to change that perception. If we're doing better than our parents, we feel like imposters. If we are doing worse, we might spend like we are in a higher financial class. Imposter syndrome is real, and it can be a beast to overcome.

For my own financial upbringing, growing up I perceived that my family and I were not well off; as a consequence, this has made me feel like an imposter at times when I'm in situations with peers who belong to higher income brackets. I do quite well for myself now and can afford things my parents only dreamed of while raising me and my brothers. But when I'm in those situations and in those rooms, I do not feel like I belong. It's ludicrous. Our worth is not defined by how we were raised or how much money we have now.

What I want you to take away from this chapter is an understanding of your own personal relationship with money and how it has been influenced by your life experiences. I won't include a journaling exercise in this chapter, but feel free to spend some time thinking about your encounters with money as you grew up and throughout your life. If you need more structure, visit my website cherishwinsor.com for some potential prompts.

Your Emotional Connection to Money

As you aged, entered the workforce, and began to pay bills, you continued to interact with money and developed more personal connections with it. You had more control, but those lessons you inadvertently learned as a child stuck with you. I don't know your story so your lessons could have been positive. Mine were not. I had several fast-food jobs, babysitting gigs, and paper routes before I became an adult. As quickly as the money came, it also left, usually being spent on junk food or wasted on some random thing I wanted.

When I was quite young, I formed my emotional connection to money, which was that money could bring me happiness by spending it on things I wanted and otherwise couldn't get. I could exercise control over my happiness, and therefore money, by earning more and spending more. The helplessness that I felt as a child fueled my need to earn money and unfortunately, spend it.

As a young teen, I worked after school in a pizza shop. It was a cash job, and I was paid every night when I went home. By the next afternoon, I'd have spent most of the money on lunch for my friends and me and would need to work another shift to earn more. By the time I was 16, this cycle led me to quit school so that I'd have more time to work. To that sixteen-year-old girl, happiness came from spending money and the only way I could continue to be happy was to earn more money. Looking back, I can see how those patterns were developed and then reinforced by my experiences.

Exercise 2 – Your Financial Persona

Your persona is the version of you that you present to others, and you might just have a few. The way you present yourself at work is likely a little different than how you act, look, feel, and present yourself when out for lunch with your friends. The individual aspects of your various personas can be the result of conscious choices you make like selecting an outfit to wear while out with your friends, or they can be unconscious like when you adopt the language and phrasing of the business world when at work. How many times have we asked our partners or friends to put a pin in something or circle back to it? Those phrases tend to be reserved for specific work environments, not our home life and we don't even notice when we switch between the two.

To take it a little further, the way you view yourself is likely a little different depending on the lens you use. Do you feel confident in your ability to manage your household but less so in a room full of strangers where you need to make small talk? Or maybe for you, it's the other way around? The way you view your abilities and knowledge of a topic can also shape the persona that we put on.

In the same way, you have a financial persona that began in childhood and has been shaped and developed throughout your life based on your experiences. Your persona is not your financial situation or current circumstances, though those will undoubtably affect the way you view money. Instead, your persona is how you approach your personal finances.

In this exercise, we're going to identify your financial persona and see how it relates to your current relationship with money. Because we are constantly learning and adapting to our environment, we are also constantly adjusting our personas to fit those variables. Whatever your persona now, the good news is that you can consciously alter it. After you've completed the exercise, take some time to think about whether it fits your current outlook and if so, consider any aspects that you would like to change or adjust.

In this exercise, you are asked to decide to what extent you agree with each of the statements listed below. You do not need to share your responses with anyone. The exercise itself is just a fun way to help you categorize your current relationship with money so that you can determine whether there are any areas that you would like to work on. It will be a little reminiscent of the quizzes we did in teen magazines, but maybe a little less fun.

If you need to skip a question (for example if you don't have a spouse), select the Unsure category.

	Strongly disagree	Disagree	Unsure /neutral	Agree	Strongly agree
1. I feel well-equipped to make financial decisions and to teach my children about money.					
2. I'd be happier if I had more money.					
3. When I buy myself something I want, I feel guilty because I could be spending my money more wisely.					
4. I feel anxious if I don't have money in the bank or a backup method to pay for things.					

5. Sometimes I hide my financial success from others because I don't want them to think I'm bragging.					
6. As a child, I was encouraged to save any money I received or earned.					
7. My parents didn't talk about money growing up.					
8. Money doesn't seem to stretch as far as I think it will. I often run out before my next paycheque.					
9. Investing isn't for me. It seems too complicated and I'm afraid I'll lose my money.					
10. My finances haven't turned out the way I thought they would when I was growing up.					
11. If I had more money, I'd use it for good.					
12. Banks and financial advisors have my best interests at heart.					
13. Money is important, but I don't spend a lot of time thinking or worrying about it.					
14. If fewer people worried about growing their personal wealth, there would be a lot more money to go around.					

15. Budgets are for poor people so that they can make their paycheques last.					
16. With the way things are going, I'll never be able to retire.					
17. My partner and I fight about money a lot. It's a huge stress in our relationship.					
18. Sometimes when I'm tired, I order takeout, then feel guilty for wasting money.					
19. I make up excuses when I'm invited out because I don't want anyone to know I'm broke.					
20. I believe I can change my current circumstances and live a financially free life.					

Scoring

For questions 1-5 give yourself these points:

Choice	Strongly disagree	Disagree	Neutral	Agree	Strongly agree
Points	1	2	3	4	5

For questions 6-7 give yourself these points:

Choice	Strongly disagree	Disagree	Neutral	Agree	Strongly agree
Points	2	1	5	3	4

For questions 8-14 give yourself these points:

Choice	Strongly disagree	Disagree	Neutral	Agree	Strongly agree
Points	5	4	3	2	1

For questions 15-20 give yourself these points:

Choice	Strongly disagree	Disagree	Neutral	Agree	Strongly agree
Points	3	4	1	5	2

Total your answers to find your financial persona:

1-20 points	21-40 points	41 to 60 points	61 to 80 points	81 to 100 points
Purple	Blue	Green	Yellow	Orange

Your Financial Persona

Purple

You're outwardly laid-back when it comes to your personal finances but secretly you know you could be doing better. You have debt and pay too much in late fees, bank fees or interest. Money allows you to have fun and spend time with friends. You can be impulsive but that helps you to be creative. You're a little cynical of the world and don't trust people with a lot of money. You avoid talking about money because it makes you uncomfortable.

Blue

You're curious about life and money but so far, you don't think you've learned much. As a result, you haven't really done anything with your money other than just live your life. You're perceptive and notice things about people that others miss. Your free spirit means you're willing to spend your money, but you do experience shame when you spend too much. As a quiet thinker, you don't talk much about money and you sometimes feel envious of others. You are likely to take small steps in life and money and want to learn more.

Green

You are comfortable when making financial decisions and follow the status quo. You were raised middle-class or above and find joy in socializing. You either have a financial planner or friends who are knowledgeable about personal finance. You own your home or have investments but don't concern yourself too much with money. You know you will be able to retire at an appropriate time but haven't thought much about financial freedom or an early retirement. While responsible and not a big risk taker, you don't mind a little bit of fun.

Yellow

Money interests you but it doesn't control you. You likely have investments or have spent some time learning about investing yourself. You think you can do better than a financial advisor. You're responsible and strategic but you're always looking for new and creative ways to build your wealth. You're an idealist with a slant to the practical. You take risks and this can lead to some tension with those around you.

Orange

You're not comfortable unless you have a backup plan for your backup plan. Money gives you comfort but it takes up a lot of your mental space and time. You are comfortable making financial decisions but still feel anxious that you won't have enough. You are strategic and know where your money is going. Your practical side doesn't leave a lot of room for risk but you're not risk-avoidant. You can be stubborn and often think you know more than others. This trait has served you well financially.

How did it feel to read your persona? Does it match how you see yourself? Parts of it likely resonated with you and maybe some did not. If you were close to scoring a different colour, perhaps you are somewhere in between.

I can say that for many years I had a purple financial persona. I always felt like I should be doing better than I was, but I blamed my circumstances, rather than my lack of knowledge for all of the debt and wasted money. I was curious about how other people seemed to do better than me but avoided learning anything, likely out of fear.

Over time, I moved more into a blue persona and was completely in that category around the time I turned thirty.

Maybe it was the impending big 3-0 birthday or maybe it was just the natural changes to my lifestyle, but I started to want more and took my first baby steps to figure out what that meant. I was just starting to form my Why and pay attention to ways I could realise it. Today, I'm more of a Yellow with a little sprinkle of orange. I have a plan; I know where my money is going and I'm more confident than I've ever been in my ability to make financial choices.

If there are aspects of your financial persona that you don't like or that are holding you back from the financial future you dream of, it's time to change that. Let go of the negative emotions and put money back where it belongs. We're going to talk a little more about how to do this later but first, we need to examine how your relationship with money is influenced by others right now.

CHAPTER 3
MONEY AND OTHERS

TLDR: Who you surround yourself with is important. Make friends with people who also desire a better financial future and grow together.

To create a more holistic picture of your financial life, we're going to explore how your relationships with friends, family and your spouse can affect your financial health and future. We're going to touch on the friends and family piece briefly before delving into the partner/spouse dynamic. This is simply because the way you and your partner approach money can have a major impact on your relationship, quality of life, and financial health.

Just as the family you grew up in and your upbringing can affect how you see money, so can your social circle. Without even knowing it, the people at work, playgroup, church, Starbucks, or the school pick-up line may all influence your spending habits and goals. When you hear that a colleague has just returned from a fabulous all-inclusive vacation, does it make you want to plan your own? When the other moms at school pick-up are wearing their Lululemon, drinking out of their Stanley cups and have perfect nails – does that make you feel like your frumpy clothes or plain nails aren't enough? Do you chat with your friends about their favourite stocks and their strategies for getting the best return on their savings accounts?

While I'm a big proponent of teaching yourself whatever it is you need to know using books, podcasts, videos, blogs, etc., there is nothing better than learning and discussing together with your social circle.

As a young mom, my friends and I were broke. We were in our early twenties and were juggling raising kids while attending university. What we had in common was a drive for a better life and our path there was through education. This also coincided with a time in my life when I knew nothing about personal finance and was racking up debt like nobody's business. In other words, I was in my purple financial persona years. Those friendships, while valuable in other ways, were not going to help me achieve a better financial future. It's not that the friendships were bad, it's that we didn't know any better and there was no one in our group to learn from.

Ten years ago, almost to the day, I was sitting at my living room computer chatting with a friend who lived in Alberta. She was one of those friends from my university days who had struggled along with me through raising young children while going to school. She had gone from being a broke university student to owning multiple homes and getting to be home with her kids most days. I didn't tell her that I was envious of how she had been able to achieve so much. Instead, because by then, I had taken on more of a blue persona, I asked for her advice. I knew I could change my life, I just needed to figure out how.

Our conversation that day focused mostly on the idea of moving my family to another province. My ex-husband and I were wallowing in our careers and with my fifth baby in my arms, I knew we needed to do something different. I wasn't yet looking for financial freedom, I just needed more balance and security than what I had at the time. We discussed the merits and job possibilities in both BC and Alberta. In the end, I didn't choose either province, but her story and our conversation inspired me and propelled me through the next six months until we finally moved.

Back then, I was focused on trying to make things work as they were. I had been self-employed before my daughter's birth so wasn't eligible for employment insurance. Instead, I took a job that I hated while her dad stayed home with her while on parental leave. We couldn't afford infant childcare, so we were just focused on getting by. Moving, especially across the country, hadn't been on my radar. But when I gave myself permission to dream and to believe in more for our lives, I could see that moving could be a good thing for my family. Other than education, that move turned out to be the biggest turning point in my financial life.

You may be feeling stuck in a rut and that you have no options. Or you may be feeling like your dreams and your Why are too far out of reach and you're not sure how you could get there. I had no idea ten years ago that by choosing to move my family to an unknown northern city, I'd be able to reach financial freedom and retire early. That wasn't even something I could have imagined at that time. But I could see that by doing something that was out of my comfort zone and taking steps towards the future I did want for my kids, I could achieve my dreams.

Fast forward a few years to when I focused on advancing my career, dabbled in politics, and became a leader in my community through my work leading charitable organizations. My social circle had changed and so had my conversations. I was now more likely to be in a boardroom discussing budgets worth millions of dollars or having a coffee while chatting about interest rates. Not only did the conversations change, but the net worth of those I was having conversations with also changed. This is obviously in part because we were older and no longer broke students but it's an example of a stark contrast between two social groups and seasons in my life.

I'm not advocating for you to ghost your book club or get a whole new social circle. Instead, I'm encouraging you to look for the people in your life who are where you want to be and maybe spend a little more time with them. Ask a colleague to go for a coffee and see what you can learn. At the next family gathering, pick your cousin's brain about their investment strategy and how they got started. If you're genuinely interested, many people will be willing to share their thoughts and you may be surprised what you'll learn.

I do have one caveat in all of this, though. Do not take advice from anyone at face value. Always do your own research and consider any advice through the lens of your own life. Just because something worked for one person, that does not guarantee it would work for someone else. There are too many variables and complexities for that. You always get the final say when it comes to your personal financial future. Remember that!

Money and Partners

If you're in a relationship with someone and you live together, you likely share finances in some way. How you approach this could be the result of watching your parents or others in your social circle, or you may have come up with a different approach based on your partner's experiences or something you read. There are nearly as many ways to manage money as there are couples in this world so I will never tell you which way is best. Your life and situation are unique to you and your partner, and you will need to decide for yourself what works best.

You may be asking why I'm writing about this at all if I don't plan to share my thoughts and that's a good question. I'm writing this section to give you a little food for thought. Your perceptions about how things should be done are likely the result of your past experiences (surprise!) and may not be the best option for you now. As a Millennial, the world you grew up in no longer exists and the way things were done likely doesn't really apply.

I won't tell you what to do anywhere in this book. Your situation is too personal and complex for me to be able to do that. What I want to do is give you the tools and information I used, so that you can make the best decisions for yourself.

As you consider these options with your partner, it will be important to keep in mind that you both have your own relationships with money and financial personas that were influenced by a myriad of experiences throughout your lives. If you don't see eye-to-eye on every detail, that's okay. Keep moving and circle back to that part when you can.

Paying Bills and Dividing Expenses

There are many ways to set up your finances and none of them are necessarily right. What works for one couple may not work for someone else. If you're thinking about moving in with someone or simply haven't had a conversation with your partner about how to divide expenses before, it's important that you find time to do so. Some of the ways that couples do this are outlined below but let me stress that there is no right or wrong way to do this. It's absolutely a personal choice with many variables.

All-in: You share a single joint account, and all of your paycheques and other cash are deposited into this account. You use it to pay for all your household expenses as well as any personal expenses. You likely have joint credit cards. You may agree on set amounts for things like personal discretionary spending or entertainment, or you may not.

All-in with a little on the side: As above, you share a joint account, but also have your own accounts. What goes into those accounts and what you do with them can vary but it is very much your own money that your partner does not have access to. This is how my current partner and I do it.

Half & half: You each have your own account and a joint account. You agree on how much money each of you deposits into the joint account on payday. You may have decided that certain expenses like your own vehicles or take-out lunches are covered by your own accounts, while shared things like your mortgage get covered by the joint account. This is how my ex-husband and I tackled our bills.

One-sided: You or your partner pay for all the household expenses and handle all the bill payments.

Down the middle: You split bills evenly down the middle. For each bill, one of you is responsible for paying it, and the other person gives them their share.

Free range: Each of you covers different household bills piecemeal according to your income or lifestyle. You may decide that because you're living in a home bought by you or your partner before you were together, it makes more sense for that person to pay the mortgage and for the other partner to cover groceries and utilities, for example.

There are more ways to divide expenses and manage money as a couple, but these are some of the most common. You and your partner can choose one of these or you can mix and match pieces to find a solution that works for both of you.

This discussion can bring up lots of other issues about determining how much to contribute to joint accounts or how to make things balanced and fair. Both of these issues are explored later. For now, we're just considering options so that you can think about your situation and decide if it's the best fit.

Who Looks After The Books?

As with banking and splitting the cost of things, who makes sure the bills get paid is also a personal decision between you and your partner. In my serious relationships, I've tended to be the person who tracks our spending and keeps an eye on things. I don't necessarily pay all the bills but I'm more likely to "manage" the money than my partners have been. My current partner, who has an orange money persona, was used to managing the money in his previous relationships, so it was a little bit of an adjustment when we moved in together and we had to learn how to work together. Some days, we're still learning.

Your situation will be unique to you but in general, couples can either pay their bills together each month, have everything set to auto-pay through pre-authorized payments with their bank or credit card, or find it easier for one person to track everything. Consider what might work in your situation and discuss it with your partner. There is no hard rule and if something doesn't work, you can always try something else.

Different circumstances also require different plans. What you do today may be different than what you do next year. Don't be afraid to reassess and adjust to continue to make things work for you.

What's Fair

See above. There's no right way to do this. Some couples will share their cost of living down the middle with each paying the same dollar amount. Some will use percentages based on how much they make. Some won't divide at all because one person is responsible for the household chores rather than the bills. It's entirely up to you and what's fair is subjective.

The only thing that matters is that you remain open with your partner and have honest discussions about how you both view your money. Regardless of the way you choose to manage it, make sure you check in with each other often. As adults, it's important that you're always both fully aware of your financial situation. Knowledge is priceless and the more you know, the better prepared you will be for anything that comes your way.

When Your Partner Won't Get On Board

Now, I know there are different personalities and dynamics in relationships and some people just don't want to discuss money at all. It is especially difficult if money is tight or if you have different views on how you should be managing your money. While you can't force anyone to do anything, you can make the space and time to try, expressing your desire and letting them know that a conversation is important to you. Whether the other person comes to the table will be up to them.

Like many couples, money was an issue in my first marriage. We didn't make enough of it, we had different goals and spending styles, and we couldn't agree on how it should be managed. Despite that, we did manage to pay off all of my ex-husband's debts and rebuild his credit. We even bought our first house together shortly before we split. The journey wasn't easy, and I often felt like I was pulling him along on a path he didn't want to be on. I was happy to achieve what we did but it was exhausting.

In my current relationship, we have monthly check-ins, quarterly finance meetings and an annual family finance meeting. But that's just because both my partner and I enjoy this stuff. During our monthly check-ins, we discuss upcoming expenses and any categories of our budget that are over or underspent. We also own a couple of businesses, so the conversations are usually a mix of business and personal. The meetings are informal and usually have us sitting in our living room one morning during the first week of each month.

Every three months (or sometimes, every six) we check in on the budget lines and categories to see if we need to adjust anything. If we're overspent in one area, we may decide to take from another category that is underspent. It's also a good time to check in on our long-term investments and review our general net worth.

Our annual family finance meeting is my favourite. At the end of each year, we gather all the kids and show them how we did with our budget. We let them see how well we stuck to our plan and then together, decide if we want to make any adjustments for the new year. This not only teaches them how to budget and the importance of it, but it also gives them some control and the ability to weigh their desires against the constraints we've put in place.

If this isn't your reality and your partner doesn't like to talk money, I encourage you to take small steps to help them open up. Don't try to overwhelm them with spreadsheets and budgets or start by discussing how far behind you are on your bills. Remember, just like you, your partner has a relationship with money and may need some support to overcome any negative emotions that they connect to it. Be patient and be open to discussing things with them. If you've tried everything and don't feel like you're making any progress, you can also try counselling. Relationship counsellors can help you and your partner to explore your emotions around money and get you communicating better.

The Power Of A Mentor

Before I end this chapter, I'd be doing you a disservice if I didn't mention the power of a mentor in your financial journey. I am a firm believer in mentorship, whether through a formal arrangement or an informal (but consistent) relationship with someone you admire.

Millennials aren't great at connecting, so the act of seeking out a mentor may be daunting. As an introvert, I have trouble connecting with others and finding meaningful relationships. Books, articles, and podcasts have taught me so much. But I've also learned to seek out friends and colleagues who I felt I could learn from, even if they didn't know they were mentoring me at the time.

About eight years ago, I found myself in a tough situation at work. My supervisor had gone on maternity leave and her position wasn't filled. Instead, I was left to do much of her work as well as mine. I felt that the arrangement was unfair, but I didn't know how to bring it up with the head of our department. I didn't want to talk to anyone that I worked with because I felt they would be too close to the issue. I also didn't know a lot of people who worked in corporate settings that I could ask for advice.

I went through my mental Rolodex, considering who I could go to and came up with one name. This was someone who I considered a friend but who I didn't know super well. He was doing amazingly in his career though and was close to my age. This was someone who had a career I could only dream of. The only problem was that I didn't know how he would respond if I asked him for career advice. We had never talked about work before.

As luck would have it, he happened to be in town around that time and we arranged to go for a hike. I saw that as my opportunity and without seeming too eager, I casually brought up my dilemma as we climbed the rocky hills surrounding a lake. I wondered aloud if I should straight out tell my department head that the situation was unfair and ask to be given an acting role. My friend was quick to point out that my tactics may backfire and only upset my boss.

Instead, he suggested that if I found a way to show them all the ways that I was supporting the goals of the department, and backed that up with real data, I'd be in a better position to ask for what I wanted. That little piece of advice has stuck with me to this day, and I still use his method. My friend didn't realize that he was mentoring me that day and I still don't think he has ever realised that was how I saw him. He was just giving me his honest opinion and I was able to use that to get compensation and recognition for my work.

Later in my career, and while working at a different company, I saw an opportunity for a promotion during a reorganization. This time, I was ready and presented my boss with my plan. I wanted to head a new department that would support the business in a way that it hadn't been. I pitched myself as the person to lead the department and showed how I would go from the position I had at the time, to this new management role. My proposal included the self-directed learning that I would commit to, but most importantly, it identified my need for a mentor.

My boss agreed to everything in the proposal, and I was given the promotion. Over the two years that followed, I made sure to hit all the targets I had outlined, and my boss held up her end of the deal. She personally selected a mentor for me that turned out to be exactly the person I needed. My mentor was encouraging and thoughtful during our monthly meetings, but she didn't hold my hand. She was a busy woman and well-respected across our global business. When we finally met in person more than a year later, she made sure to take the time to talk with me, even though she was incredibly busy.

If finding a mentor is too much for you right now, I encourage you to seek out books, online communities, or podcasts that can give you something like mentorship, though not quite as personal. Heck, even this book can help in some ways. I don't pretend to know all the answers, but I hope I can be a helpful friend that you can confide in and share your dreams with. I promise not to judge and to have your back.

At the end of this book, you'll find an offer for one-on-one coaching from me. If you're interested, you can find the offer on page 133 or visit my website for details.

CHAPTER 4
MINDSET

TLDR: To really thrive, you need to get out of survival mode and build the life you want to live right now. Knowing what you want and believing that you can achieve it is half the battle. Regardless of how you were raised and where you come from, you are worthy of your dreams.

I may not have learned a lot of positive money management tools growing up, but my parents instilled in me a strong belief in myself. I'm definitely not the most confident person and I've certainly struggled with self-esteem at times, but I do know that I can do whatever it is that I want in life and that gift has allowed me to live with intention and purpose.

The only thing stopping me from achieving my dreams or goals is myself. Of course, there are all sorts of outside pressures to contend with. But at the root of it all, it is my belief in myself that has allowed me to do things that others have been too scared to try.

I wouldn't have had the confidence to make the choices that got me where I am today if it weren't for those lessons of worth that my mother poured into me. Never once did I doubt my ability to succeed. Even when the job offers weren't coming in or when we put all our belongings in storage and packed our minivan with five kids to move across the country. I didn't even fold when some of our closest friends told us we would fail. I knew this path was right for our family and I was determined to see it through, all thanks to my positive mindset.

Keeping a Positive Mindset

I considered titling this section something along the lines of following your intuition or trusting yourself to make big decisions. In the end, I settled on Keeping a Positive Mindset because a) it's a little less hippy-dippy and b) I don't know you or where you're coming from, but we could likely all be a little more positive in our thinking. Suffice it to say, the next few paragraphs are a little bit of all three.

In earlier chapters, we discussed the influence that your upbringing, social circle, and your past experiences had on your relationship with money. The same is true when it comes to how you view yourself. I hope you have had people to build you up and fill you with confidence and strength. But if that hasn't been your story, I want you to know that you are worthy and valued. You have so much to give the world and yourself.

If this mindset isn't something you're used to, it can be tough to trust yourself to make the right choices; to drown out the world and listen to that inner voice. The good news is that you can, even if you're a purple or blue persona person. It just takes practice.

Your intuition, or your inner voice, is your guide in life and you need to learn to trust it, if you don't already. Think about it. You would never intentionally lead yourself astray. Your intuition is the part of you that wants you to succeed and isn't swayed by the nay-sayers, or your own guilt and anxiety. It knows what's right for you. Other people, while they can give their advice or opinions, will not have to live with the outcome of your decisions.

If I had ignored my inner voice and listened to all the nay-sayers, I would never have moved across the country or have the life I have today. Plain and simple. It is because I trusted myself, didn't give in to fear, and was confident in my decision-making that I can share my story with you.

The next time you are faced with a semi-difficult decision, take a step back from the opinions of others and spend some time thinking about the issue yourself. If journaling helps you, write out your thoughts. It isn't so much about what you write but about giving yourself time and permission to consider the issue and sit with it for a while. If you listen to what that inner voice is telling you, you'll likely be leaning more toward one direction over the other. Let your intuition guide you.

Don't just consider the pros and cons of it. Instead, try to work through the reasons you're doubting yourself and not just conceding to what you know is the right choice. It may be that there will be consequences that you don't like or that you are scared to move in that direction. If you quiet the voices, even your own doubts, you might be surprised how clear your decision will be. Try it and let me know how it goes.

Doing Hard Things

Years ago, when I was preparing for my move across the country, I had a friend who was in a similar financial situation. We both had degrees and were raising young kids. Neither of us were able to find work in our chosen fields and we were working horrible jobs just trying to get by.

Nearly every time I saw this friend, I would tell her about some aspect of my upcoming move or the jobs I was applying for. We discussed the number of job openings in our fields and the much higher salaries then were possible where we lived. We talked about other similar locations and the possibilities they held. We even discussed what it might look like if things didn't turn out and I ended up in an even worse financial situation.

Throughout our conversations, I tried time and again to convince her of the merits of a similar move for her and her family. I could see how much better she would be doing if she left her home province and followed the work. Her kids weren't yet in school, and it seemed like a great time. There were plenty of available jobs for both her and her husband and it seemed like a no-brainer to me.

Nearly every time though, she would say it wasn't for her. She was too scared to do it. There were too many ways it could go wrong, and it seemed like too big of a change. There were so many excuses, it was clear I would never convince her. We've mostly lost touch but from what I've seen on social media, not much has changed for her in these past 10 years; in contrast, the person I was ten years ago would never be able to recognize my life as it is today.

Some might say that my friend was right to make the choice she did and that it showed confidence in herself and her decision-making. I might even agree with you. The part of our conversations that I feel was missing was her reasoning. Not just a simple kneejerk reaction to something that seems crazy, but her real reasoning as well as mine. I can't remember if I ever told her my Why, but I know I didn't ask what hers was.

I've often thought of my friend these last few years and whether moving would have been as lucrative for her as it was for me. I could give her my opinion, but only she knew what was right for her and her family. What worked for me may not have worked for her. Still, if she had taken the time to sit and consider a move, she may have been able to identify the reason for her choice. She may have been scared because things would be different than what she was used to, or she may have identified that being close to family was more important to her. An informed choice is always better than one made from fear.

Striving Isn't Thriving

From the time we are young, we are always working towards something. We learn to crawl, walk, and run. We learn to speak, read, and write. We earn diplomas and maybe even degrees. We earn money from babysitting, odd jobs, or paper routes before we work in fast food, retail, or service jobs. We start our entry-level jobs and work our way up the corporate ladder. We save for toys, clothes, and school, then houses, vacations, and retirement. We buy our first homes and then trade up to bigger and bigger houses. The striving for more never really ends.

To really thrive, you need to stop chasing what you are supposed to want and instead purposefully build a life you want to live right now.

Only you know your dreams and can define your Why, so I won't tell you what thriving looks like for you. For me, I knew I didn't want to be told what to do every day at work. I enjoyed my work, but I craved my freedom and the four walls of my office started to feel like a prison. While I celebrated every one of my promotions, climbing the corporate ladder didn't give me pleasure. It meant more work and more demands on the little time I had. With each promotion, I saw little bits of my freedom break away.

On top of the pressures to succeed, Millennial women are plagued by burnout and exhaustion. We're depressed and working too hard for rewards we aren't even sure we want. I was so busy building this life I thought I was supposed to want, that I didn't even notice I wasn't thriving. It wasn't until I had made it to the executive ranks in my career and had an expensive house overlooking a lake with a second home in another province, that I realised I didn't want the stress and pressure that came with it. I didn't want to be away from my kids, spending my time focused on a business that wouldn't even exist by the time my youngest went to high school.

What I wanted was to spend my time each day doing things that I enjoyed. That could mean work; but only if the work I was doing was enjoyable and on my schedule. It could also mean being home when my daughter got off the school bus, so that I could greet her with a hot chocolate and homemade cookies. To me, that's thriving; getting to do whatever it is that I want and enjoy, but on my schedule.

Being Ready

I'm a practical sort of person so thinking positively and having confidence in myself is all well and good, but figuring out how to get from where I was to where I am now, is what I needed to understand. You're probably thinking the same thing.

I know it may not seem like it, but getting the right mindset is one of the hardest parts of this journey. Without it, and by giving into limiting thoughts and beliefs, you won't learn to recognize or evaluate an opportunity when it arrives. You might see things through a lens of fear, or you might second-guess yourself until the opportunity passes.

Knowing what you want and believing that you can achieve it is half the battle. The rest comes down to being ready when presented with an opportunity and taking steps towards your goals while you wait.

I can't promise that everything will work out as you plan because that's just life. What I can say is that when you open yourself up to the possibility of a better future, you begin to see more opportunities. Even more, when you live intentionally and begin to take steps toward your goals, you build your confidence and start to see yourself as someone who can achieve your dreams.

So, that's it. You now know what you need to build the foundation of your financially free future. Through explorations into your past relationship and history with money, your upbringing and social circle and your mindset, we've begun to unpack what's led to your current financial outlook. Armed with this information, and coupled with your Why, your path to financial freedom is becoming clearer.

In the next section, we will learn more about personal finance and consider opportunities for earning more income, reducing debt, and getting better at saving. These practical skills and knowledge can help to give you the tools you will need to develop your roadmap to your future. Then, in the last section, we will bring everything together and build that roadmap.

SECTION

Two

DITCH THE GIRL MATH AND LEARN THE REAL MONEY TOOLS YOU NEED TO BUILD THE FUTURE YOU WANT

CHAPTER 5
THE 3 BASICS OF MONEY MANAGEMENT – BUDGETING, SAVING AND DEBT REPAYMENT

TLDR: Before you budget, figure out where your money is going now. Savings are important but don't bother building the emergency fund if you have consumer debt.

We've all heard of "girl math" on social media. Every time I see a video or hear a woman make a joke about this ridiculous trend, I cringe. Most of the jokes are from people who I assume have a blue or green financial persona, and rather than educating themselves about finances, they play along with a trend that makes women sound frivolous. A lot of us, regardless of gender, feel as though we should know more about finance and money than we actually do. So instead of playing along with the stereotype, confront your feelings and take steps to learn what you need for a financially free future.

I've heard so many women shame themselves because they're not where they want to be financially. If that's you, just stop right now. There is absolutely no shame in learning something new. We all have to start somewhere and I'm proud of you for taking the time to learn what you need to have the life you want.

Over the next few chapters, I'm going to cover the basics of personal finance and dive a little deeper into a few key topics so that we can all learn together. I know some of this will be a refresher for some and brand new for others. If there are areas you are super interested in or need more information about, I encourage you to visit my website Cherishwinsor.com where I share additional resources.

Budgeting Basics

It's no secret that to fully understand your finances, you should have a budget. I've never been as big on budgets as I have been on tracking my spending. To make a good budget, you first need to know where your money is going; budgeting your money, or telling it where to go, is the second step.

When my partner and I moved in together and blended our families, we were coming from different perspectives in terms of budgeting and spending. We didn't know how to divide the expenses or where to even start. So, for the first six months, we just tracked our spending without making a budget. Being someone who has had many budgets over the years, it felt weird not to have one, but an important exercise because it showed us our spending habits as a couple and a new family.

Step One: Track your Expenses

Even if you already have a budget, I recommend taking the time to track your real expenses. This means writing down everything you spend, from the couple of dollars you put in the parking meter to the rent or mortgage you pay. Six months isn't very long but it will give you so much insight into your spending habits. You'll also be committing to take the first step in understanding your finances and creating the future you want.

For me, I used a good old-fashioned spreadsheet where I manually added expenses each month into categories. We have both personal and joint credit cards and bank accounts and I found manually entering the data to be a good way to review every expense. If you're less impressed by spreadsheets, you may choose to use a free or paid app or online tool. I don't use either so have no personal recommendations to share but encourage you to do a quick search for one if this would interest you. Whichever method you choose, the important thing is to commit to it and to make sure you do it.

If you put it off, not only will you miss out on all of that info, but you'll probably also feel frustrated for having something else on your to-do list that you're not getting done. Even if it's only for three months, do it and I promise, you will be surprised to learn where your money goes.

I had no idea that we spent as much on take-out or alcohol as we did, *ahem*. I was also surprised that our pets ended up costing much less than I expected (we had two cats and two dogs at the time). If you want to use a spreadsheet like I did, or put pen to paper, just list out the overarching categories you think you spend money in. Here's an example:

	Monthly Budget	January	February	March	April	May	June	Semi-annual total spend	Semi-annnual budget
Groceries/househol	1600	1491.44	887.15	2026.34	1959.2	1351.4	2117.67	9833.24	9600
Takeout	600	558.52	545.37	1309.81	1479.5	2073.37	1426.67	7393.24	3600
Alcohol	300	596.58	170.68	304.66	455.12	482.54	356.01	2365.59	1800
Gas	200	152.15	0	332.95	354.45	150	211.9	1201.45	1200
Power	300	453.83	428.44	404.05	431.09	338.78	307.11	2363.3	1800
Internet	225	225	381.99	211.99	247.67	253.96	253.96	1574.57	1350
Water	150	151.18	113.12	146.12	161.2	148.53	155.36	875.51	900
Misc shopping	200	104.95	0	465.59	455.79	508.43	253.16	1787.92	1200
Travel	1050	111.92	47.99	2076.02	1475.45	3146.89	4921.44	11779.71	6300
Vet / Pets	100	0	0	0	0	0	0	0	600
Credit card interest	50	143.3	156.75	100.21	0	179.73	140.33	720.32	300
Mortgatge	2450	2346.74	2346.74	2346.74	3520.11	2346.74	2346.74	15253.81	14700
Vehicles	1650	1293.1	1293.1	1293.1	1939.65	1293.1	1293.1	8405.15	9900
Insurance	335	0	0	0	0	0	0	0	2010
Propane	300	1047.78	0	318.02	762.06	228.72	266.79	2621.97	1800
Taxes	585	0	0	3327.75	0	0	0	3327.75	3510
Toys	600	0	0	150.59	0	0	0	150.59	3600
Charity	50	0	0	170	0	0	0	170	300
Activities	100	90	0	93.2	320	426.83	365.9	1295.93	600
Home Maintenance	150	189	0		16.5	562.33	22.45	790.28	900
Gifts	350	0	13.04	42.53	1182.09	203.38	208.59	1649.63	2100
Monthly Totals	11345	8955.49	5384.41	15119.67	14760.48	13692.73	14647.18		

A real screenshot of my family financial tracker from a few years ago. Note, this is a financial tracker and not a typical budget.

Get this Template and Guide from my website
Cherishwinsor.com

Yours can look similar, though, your numbers will be different, or you can change it to suit your spending categories. It's okay to have an "other" category, but if you find that you're putting a lot of things in there, it would be better to give those things their own category so that you can be more accurate. What's important with this format is to record your true spending numbers, regardless of whether they match your budgeted or expected spend. I use red numbers to indicate all the times we went over budget, while green indicates where we underspent. The two columns on the right compare our actual spending over six months to our expected spend.

For each month, repeat the same categories in a new column or on a new page and track those. At the end of each month, add up what you've spent in each category. Do this again by adding together your totals from the first three months and again at the six-month mark.

Because I don't want you to stop reading this book for six months while you track your spending, I'll walk through the steps to follow and encourage you to refer to these throughout the coming months if you have questions. It will also be a good idea to re-read this section once you've had a chance to read through the rest of the chapters, especially those about savings, to make sure you are budgeting for those. Of course, if you don't use much cash, you can probably go back and find six months of data from your credit card and bank statements. Be careful if you do this however, as many of us do use some cash and your data is only as accurate as you are.

Step Two: Review Your Data

Once you've tracked your spending, your next job is to review the data and decide if your current spending aligns with your values and goals or if there are areas that need attention. For us, we had to decide whether cutting down on takeout food and cooking at home instead would better suit our goals. Our answer was a yes and no.

We didn't want to spend as much as we had on takeout, but we also had very busy jobs and lives that kept us out of the kitchen. Our compromise was to limit takeout for the family to once per week while still buying the odd lunch out while working. This is the beauty of having the data available. It gave us a starting point to understand where our money was going and then align it to our lifestyle and goals.

Remember that family budget meeting and monthly check-in with my partner? This is when we have these conversations. For our first meeting after blending our families, we screen-shared my laptop to a large TV and went line by line over our spending. Then we gave the kids (ranging from 8 to 20) a total budget and asked them to suggest how they wanted it spent. They could see that we spent more for example on entertainment (travel and recreational activities) than on our transportation, and they knew that if they wanted to increase or decrease those, there would be compromises.

Of course, we had the final say and vetoed a couple of their ideas but in the end, they chose to increase our travel and entertainment categories (of course) and reduce our takeout and grocery spending. Now, when they want those treats at the grocery store, I can remind them of their choices. This also allowed us to upgrade our family vacation last year to top-tier accommodations and VIP amenities.

Step Three: Budgeting Based on Data

Once you've reviewed your spending and reconciled the data with your lifestyle and goals, you will need to decide where you'd like your money to go. Add up the total for each category after six months and divide by six. This will give you your average monthly spend for that category. If the number doesn't feel right for that category or you saw some things in step two that you want to address, now's the time to make those changes.

It could be as simple as deciding to reduce your grocery or household supply category while increasing your vehicle maintenance category. Ask yourself if you've included everything or if there's a category missing. Are there big annual expenses that you could plan for rather than trying to pay them when they come up?

We will get more into emergency planning and retirement or savings accounts later but for now, your job is to think about the categories you may want to include, even if you don't yet know the specifics. Remember, money isn't just something that comes and goes in your life. You can use it and harness it to create the lifestyle you want. This is why a budget is such an important place to start.

You may not have noticed you were doing it, but you've now created a budget. If you followed the steps above, you've laid out your future spending plan, based on your real spending habits and informed by your financial goals and lifestyle. Congratulations! That was a big first step.

Making Ends Meet

You may have found that your total spend each month is higher than your income. Don't worry, this is true for so many of us. Remember that Millennials on average have $50,000 in unsecured debt. This is part of the reason why.

Of course, you eventually want to have money left over every month but if that's not happening, try not to get too discouraged. Learning how to build a budget and understanding where your money is going is like the key that opens the door to your future. Once you're comfortable with your budget, you will know what you can trim or where you need to make edits. Plus, we will talk more about debt and earning extra income later, so we can consider how those affect your budget then.

I'm not here to police you and in a way, neither are you. I believe budgets are meant to be fluid so that they can change and adapt as you learn and as your lifestyle changes. A static hard-set budget might be for some people but for most of us, we need a little flexibility in our lives.

Savings

Your circumstances can often dictate your financial priorities, regardless of whether you have a budget. Sometimes, there's just not enough money to go around and you have less control over where and what you spend. Your circumstances, or the people you surround yourself with, can also dictate your wants and have you spending your hard-earned money on things you didn't plan for.

Have you ever noticed family members or friends who are in debt or have a low income, tend to always wear brand-name clothes or shoes, carry expensive handbags, or buy the latest iPhone? I'm sure you know a few people like this, or maybe you are one yourself. You may ask yourself how they can afford those things and the answer is, they can't. They are financing a lifestyle above their means through debt and bad money management.

In principle, it's okay to want to fit in and feel that you're like everyone else. There's nothing wrong with that. When you can't afford something, it feels like everyone else has it and you're missing out. You think that if you could just have that nice purse, big house, or dress better, you would feel more like everyone else. I get it, but if this is you, this purple persona mindset will keep you down. You spend what little money you have, or you go into debt to fund a lifestyle that is beyond your means, only to end up with higher interest rates or missed payments and a lower credit score.

I'm telling you, there's a better way.

Next to budgeting, learning to build savings is arguably the most important practical skill you can learn to set yourself up for a financially free future. For far too long, I didn't understand the value of savings and, as a consequence, I lost out on the magic that can happen when you add compound growth to long-term savings. But I'm getting ahead of myself. Let me start with this little nugget of advice instead: saving means investing. Maybe I'll say it a little louder for the people in the back, SAVING MEANS INVESTING!

When it comes to saving, you will hear time and time again that you should start with a goal, or plan for what you're saving for. That knowing what you want to spend your money on or how much you want to save, will help you do it. While this will probably help some goal-oriented folks, I think of savings a little differently.

The end goal of saving should never be to spend it. Instead, your goal should be to build wealth and to use that wealth to fund the things you want. Don't just save money for a vacation and then spend it on the vacation. That will get you right back to where you started, although probably more tanned.

Your goal should instead be to build your wealth so that your money earns growth (interest, appreciation, or dividends), or in other words, what you need to take that vacation. The idea is that your money still belongs to you, *and* you get to take that vacation. This is how you build a financially free future without having to miss out on life in the meantime.

Here's how it works. Say you want to buy yourself a designer handbag. The bag costs $5,000. You can either save $5,000 in a regular savings account and then spend it on the bag, leaving you with exactly zero dollars to put in that bag. Or you can invest $5,000, let that grow to $10,000 through interest, appreciation, or dividends, then purchase the bag and still have $5,000.

The naysayers will immediately point out that it will take much longer to get the bag that way, and they would be right. But remember what we learned in the last chapter about mindset? Once you start thinking about money the right way, you begin to prepare yourself for opportunities that allow you to grow your wealth. Being patient and, if necessary, foregoing some things you want now, will give you the freedom and ability to have what you want in the future. If you had that mindset a few years ago, you might already have the money today for that handbag.

The other Negative Nellies will tell you that you can only expect to earn around 8-10% per year on your investments, and that's keeping in mind that there are good years and bad years. I'm here to tell you that those limiting beliefs are what keep so many people from achieving their wealth potential.

In the next chapter, I'll show you exactly how I turned a $30,000 investment into $170,000 over three years. I'll also discuss how I increased my income by an average of 100% every single year of my thirties, allowing me to afford investments like this. I can buy a lot more handbags with $170,000 than I can with $30,000. I can also afford to make a lot more $30,000 investments with a quarter-million-dollar income than I could when I made less than a tenth of that.

If you're just starting out, these numbers may seem impossibly out of reach to you. A few years ago, I'd have agreed with you. Remember, this didn't happen overnight for me and it likely won't for you either. What's important to remember is that you can realise numbers like this and achieve financial freedom. You just need to be committed to shifting your mindset, stepping out of your comfort zone and putting in the work.

So how exactly do you start saving? Well, that depends on a lot of personal factors. To get started, here's a few questions to ask yourself:

- After bills, does your budget allow for any money that can be used for investments?
- Do you have debts that should be paid down first?
- Can you earn more money that can be earmarked for investments?
- Do you have access to money that's not earning up to its potential?

If you followed the budgeting exercise, you know (or will soon know) the answer to the first question and we'll discuss debt and earning more money soon.

Personally, since I was just transitioning into a yellow financial persona, that last question was what really changed things around for me. When I changed my mindset and started looking for money, I was surprised at how many avenues I had available to me. I'll share a few, but keep in mind that my situation was unique to me and your opportunities will be different:

First, my employer offered an interesting perk because I live in a remote city. To encourage leaders to stay with the company, they offered a $15,000 bonus to go towards the purchase of a home. Like everything, there were some caveats in accepting the money. But for me, someone who already owned my home, it was a great opportunity to gain funding to buy an investment property. Now this type of bonus isn't very common but it's an example of a unique and creative way to grow wealth that I hadn't even realised was available to me until I looked for it.

This next example will be more common for some readers. I receive a small amount of child support from my boys' dad. I won't get into the details but trust me when I say it's a small amount. Because his payments are so small, I set up an online High-Interest Savings Account (HISA) and had his payments go directly into that. Then, whenever the account reaches $5,000, I invest it in a 12-month Guaranteed Investment Certificate or GIC. The GICs mature at different times of the year so every few months, I have access to that cash to pull it out or reinvest.

This account became my kids "adulting fund." I don't believe post-secondary is the only choice for kids today, so I encourage them to try different things. This fund is there for either school, a house down payment, learning a new skill, or whatever else they come up with. I gave one of my young adult children $1,000 to try his hand at stock market investing because he was interested in it. Another child needed help with rent for a bit. A third is planning on buying his first home later this year and I'll be able to help him with closing costs. This money, which could have been lost in my monthly cash flow, was instead given a job to provide money as my kids learn to become adults and is generating additional wealth through an interest-generating account. The money already existed. All I did was change the way I looked at it.

These examples also illustrate two approaches to savings (AKA investing). In the first example, I allocated a lump sum to a specific investment. This is my preferred method because it is the easiest to both do and track. Other lump sums that you could use with this approach are tax returns, annual bonuses, or even cash gifts from your wedding.

The second approach involves setting aside an amount of money at regular intervals. In the example I shared, I used my child support. You could do the same thing with a paycheque, income from a side-hustle, or government payments like the Canada Child Tax Credit or GST rebates.

Money exists all around us and in more abundance than we realize. When we start to look for it and view it as a potential wealth builder, we get more out of it and can grow it into whatever we want. I encourage you to spend some time thinking about how your money flows to you and away from you and whether there are pockets of money that can be reassigned to grow your wealth.

High-Interest Savings Accounts

I always assumed that the savings account offered at my brick-and-mortar bank was just like any other and would earn me interest. When I took the time to look, I learned I was earning less than a tenth of a percent in interest. Thanks to inflation, that means my money was losing value at an alarming rate.

It's okay to keep your money in a savings account if you need access to it or need to protect it from the ups and downs of some investments. There are just some things you don't want to risk. However, keep in mind that the account should provide a decent return. These are called High-Interest Savings Accounts, and you need to specifically request or look for one.

In 2024, that means an account with an interest rate of at least 4% annually, but I'd try to look for 5% or more.

When choosing an account, make sure you shop around. Banks often offer deals to open a new account but be sure to read the fine print. Often, those deals are introductory offers, or they require you to keep a minimum amount in the account or set up direct deposits and automatic payments.

Compound Growth

If savings = investing, then we should also talk about compound growth. Because most of my wealth was accumulated in other ways, I don't like to use the term compound interest. Even though it's more common and you'll hear it more often, I find it too narrow. For me, compound growth fits better.

The money that you use to invest is called your principal and the amount you earn, either via interest, appreciation, or dividends, is your growth. To keep things simple, let's just consider interest for a moment. If you deposit $1,000 in a HISA with a 5% annual interest rate, after one year, you will have $1,050. Then, in year two, if your interest rate remains at 5%, you will gain interest on both your principal amount of $1,000 as well as your interest of $50. At the end of the second year, you would now have $1,102.50. In this example, you earned $2.50 in compound interest. That's free money, earning free money. Imagine just how effective this is when applied to large amounts of money over time!

Retirement Planning

As a generation, our retirement planning could use some work. Whether because we don't believe we will be able to retire, or because we don't know how to save for it, two-thirds of Canadian Millennials have decided to prioritize other financial goals and forego retirement saving.[7]

For many of us, it just makes sense to prioritize our debt and current lifestyle over our futures because we've bought into the idea that retirement is unachievable. I used to believe this until I started learning about compound growth and the power of a long-term savings horizon. I remember specifically thinking that I would have time to save for retirement later but that my kids were only going to be small for so long and paying for our lifestyle while saving for their education needed to be my priority. I just didn't understand savings and thought that time would come later. Those were some of my limiting beliefs, and they were just plain wrong.

What I didn't understand was the value of compound growth and the satisfaction that comes from knowing that you have that little nest egg. Money grows. Maybe not on trees but if you put it in the right spot and give it what it needs, it will grow – just like a tree.

I've had to forgive myself for those wasted years and limiting beliefs and instead focus on the future.

Retirement planning can be complex, and it's very dependent on your situation. Factors depend upon the number of years that you have to work on a plan, how much money you have access to during those years, your risk tolerance, whether your employer offers retirement plans, your retirement lifestyle goals, whether or not you have a partner, and what province or territory you live in; all of these affect your personal retirement plan. Because of this, I can't offer loads of wisdom in just this section.

What I can suggest is that you read through the rest of this book and follow the advice that works for you. Then, when you've adjusted your mindset and taken steps towards your financially free future, you can begin to develop a more structured plan specifically for retirement.

Emergency Funds

I can't tell you the number of times I've heard that building an emergency fund should be your first focus when learning about personal finance. The people behind most personal finance books, podcasts, articles, blogs, or social media groups will practically fall off their chairs trying to tell you this is a must. I disagree.

Aside from reviewing your spending and building a budget, which is the true first step, your second step should be debt repayment. Here's why:

A good emergency fund should contain 3-6 months of expenses, or 6 – 12 months for a healthy one. How long would it take you to save that? Most of us don't have 50% of our paycheques left over each month which suggests it would take a significant amount of time to reach those amounts. Even if that money is invested, your return for one year would be minimal since the idea is to keep the money in your emergency fund accessible. The often-spouted advice is to pay only your minimum required payments while you build your emergency fund, or at least part of it. But that doesn't make sense. Let me explain:

In a single year, if you maintain an average of $10,000 in credit card debt with an interest rate of 28%, you're paying $2,792, just in interest. That's lost money that could have been better spent. Instead of focusing on that emergency fund, if you spent time paying down your credit card debt, you would instead increase your wealth through lower interest payments. You could then apply that money to your emergency fund instead.

Here are some examples to help illustrate this concept better:

Monthly expenses	$5,000
Emergency fund target (6x monthly expenses)	$30,000

Budgeted monthly amount for savings or debt payments	$500
Average credit card balance	$10,000
Minimum monthly payment	$250

To keep it simple, these calculations don't account for any interest you would earn on your savings. Given that the money would need to be accessible and the volatility of some other investment types, you would likely only earn about 4% on it in a HISA so the difference isn't material.

Sarah wants to build her emergency fund first. While making minimum payments on her credit cards, it would take her ten years to save six months of expenses. That's a long time and the kicker is she would still have that $10,000 in credit card debt that would take almost another 2.5 years to pay off!

Jess instead wants to put their entire $500 towards paying off their credit card debt each month. Because of the bigger payments, they would pay off their balance in less than 2.5 years. Then, because they would be able to put twice as much towards their emergency fund, they would build six months of expenses in five years, letting them reach their savings goal, and be debt-free about 5 years earlier.

You may be asking if the advantages of paying debt first are so obvious, why do so many people advise building an emergency fund first? The answer comes down to human behaviour. It can be hard for many of us who have developed negative connections to money and bad money management skills to refrain from spending beyond our means. If we start paying down our credit card debt, we may be more likely to use our cards for purchases because we suddenly have more credit available to us.

There's also the potential that an actual emergency does happen, and you need access to emergency funding. Without anything saved in an emergency fund, you are more likely to take on debt, and at potentially higher interest rates than if you had the money already.

So then, is there a happy middle-ground? Perhaps. Using the same numbers as above, **Megan** wants to have some money put aside for emergencies and will pay off her credit card later. To save a three-month emergency fund, while making minimum credit card payments, she would reach her goal in five years, then would need another 2.5 years to pay her credit card debt. With an additional 2.5 years of saving, she would have six months of expenses saved and no credit card debt. For some folks, this could be a good compromise.

My issue with this approach, regardless of your savings target, is that it is all built on the *potential* of an emergency happening. There's no guarantee that you will need it, but if you have debt, you are guaranteed to be paying interest now. So why gamble on a potential when you have a sure thing in front of you?

Let's take a moment to look at the numbers should an emergency happen. Let's say that our example folks end up with an unexpected vehicle repair eighteen months after they started their savings/debt repayment plans. **Sarah and Megan** would have $4,500 available in their emergency funds to pay for it. **Jess** would have no savings but by paying off $4,118 in credit card debt, they have that amount available in credit. So far, both **Sarah and Megan** are looking a little smug.

But let's look closer.

After paying their $3,000 repair bill, **Sarah and Megan** are left with $1,500 in savings and **Jess** now has a balance of $8,882 in credit card debt. They will now reach their goals later, but how much later might surprise you:

> **Sarah**: was 12 years, 4 months; now becomes 13 years, 4 months

Jess: was 7 years, 4 months; now becomes 8 years, 6 months

Megan: was 9 years, 9 months; now becomes 10 years, 9 months

A simple car repair added at least a year for each of them! Even though it seems like **Sarah and Megan** would have more money available at the time of the emergency, when you look at how much longer it will take them to reach their goals, paying their debt first still makes more financial sense.

Let's do another one. Say our example folks are lucky and they don't have any emergencies for the first three years. Just after the three-year mark, their washing machines break and need replacing. Given the age of their dryers, they decide to replace those too and find a good deal by purchasing both together. They each take $2,000 from their emergency fund for the purchase and delivery.

By this point, **Sarah and Megan** have both saved $9,000 in their emergency fund and can easily cover the cost. **Jess** has now fully paid off their credit card and has not added additional debt. They also began saving in their emergency fund once their credit card reached a zero balance. So far, they have $4,000 saved. Again, they can easily cover the cost of their new washer and dryer.

While all three can cover this expense, their timelines now look like this:

Sarah: was 12 years, 4 months; now becomes 13 years

Jess: was 7 years, 4 months; now becomes 7 years, 8 months

Megan: was 9 years, 9 months; now becomes 10 years, 5 months

Not only does **Jess** still end up reaching their goals much faster than the others, but their unplanned purchase also only added 4 months to their timeline, rather than 8 months like the others.

Of course, there are bigger emergencies like a lay-off from work or a major health concern that keeps you from working. These are difficult life events, and an emergency fund will help you cover those costs. But keep in mind that if you have debt as we discussed above, you would still be responsible for paying those minimums. This could add a lot of unnecessary pressure on your bank account if you're already struggling to make ends meet. Again, removing the debt can help ease the burden.

Emergency Planning

Despite all of this, I still believe everyone should have an emergency plan. Yours could involve the use of a credit card, like Jess did in the first example. It could also mean discussing your debt repayment plan with a family member who agrees to lend you money should you have an emergency during those first few years. A third option could be to access the equity in your home through a Home Equity Line of Credit (HELOC). The point is that while it is important to have a plan to deal with the unexpected in life, debt repayment should take priority over savings. We'll discuss next what that looks like.

Debt Repayment

Debt repayment is relatively straightforward and there are a few ways to tackle it. What's best for you will depend on your personality, how you view progress and your personal situation and relationships.

Before we get into some debt repayment strategies, let's first talk about interest rates. Each of your debts likely have an interest rate attached to it. Credit cards, lines of credit, car, payday or student loans, and mortgages, all charge interest, and many charge fees in addition to the interest. The interest rate can vary and is often lower for some types of debt like mortgages or lines of credit, or higher for consumer debt like credit cards. The highest interest rates are usually found on predatory payday loans.

Your interest rate is usually listed as a percentage and can either be static, which means it stays the same or it can vary from month to month, called a variable rate. The listed percentage is the annual rate, even though you will likely be charged monthly.

Usually if you have a variable rate, it will be based on "prime" plus a few additional percentage points. Without making this too complicated, banks basically set the prime rate, which is the best possible rate they offer their best clients. Most people won't be offered this interest rate though, and instead you will be shown a number like this: Prime @ X% + X% = interest rate.

More important than the type of interest you are charged, is to know how much your interest rate is for each of your debts. If it's helpful, take some time, probably less than thirty minutes, and list all your debts. Include the current amount owing, the minimum payment amount and the interest rate. These numbers will be important when determining how to pay off those debts. If you have a mortgage or a car loan, it's okay to leave those off for now because they have set terms.

If paying them down faster is something you are interested in, and you have all other debts already paid off, I encourage you to explore these opportunities.

From your budget exercise, you should know how much money you have available for debt repayment. If that number right now is zero, that's okay. The next chapter is all about increasing your income. If you do have some money available to start paying down debt, how do you know which to tackle first? Or maybe you should spread out your payments and pay a little on all of them? Well, there are two main schools of thought when it comes to debt repayment strategies; you either pay up or you pay down.

Paying Up

Look at your list of debts and order them from the smallest amount owing to the largest. Next, add up your total minimum monthly payments for all your debts. If the amount you have available from your budget is larger than your total minimum monthly payments combined, you would pay those minimums, then put everything you have left over onto the smallest debt. With this method, you would continue to do the same each month until that smallest debt is paid off. Then, continuing up to the highest balance, you pay each debt off one-by-one.

This type of debt repayment will work best for people who need those more frequent small wins to stay motivated. Because you can watch those debts reduce and then disappear faster in the beginning, you have a chance to build up your debt repayment skills while getting more frequent dopamine hits. If you have a purple, blue or green debt persona, this could be a method that would work for you.

Paying Down

The pay down method is comparable to the paying up method but this one requires a little more math. For each of your debts, rather than just looking at the current balance, instead, take note of both the interest rate and any fees you might be paying. Calculate how much you are paying each month in both interest and fees. This is what your debts are truly costing you each month.

Following the same exercise as above, if you were to pay your minimum monthly payments on all of your debts, how much would you have left over for debt repayment? In the paying down debt method, you would apply all of that leftover money to pay down the debt that costs you the most money each month, regardless of the balance. Because of varying interest rates and fees, some debts will cost you more each month. This method is likely better for yellow or orange persona types but can be useful for anyone to try.

Which method do you think would work best for you? If you're in a relationship, does your partner agree? There's no wrong answer but it's something to ponder. If you're having trouble deciding between the two, maybe find a happy middle-ground by using a hybrid system where you pay both small debts and higher-costing debts first. Whichever method you choose, know that you can change it as you go until you find the way that works best for you.

A Note About Momentum

When you start your debt repayment, you'll work through all sorts of emotions that range from stress over how much debt you may have accumulated, to pride when you pay off a debt. As you commit to your plan and pay off more debts, you may find yourself in a groove and have no trouble continuing until you're debt-free. For many of us, that won't be the case and we start to feel the momentum wane as the debts get bigger and the timeline to being debt-free stretches long in front of us. If this is you, it'll be important to find ways to remind yourself of your Why and keep yourself motivated.

One trick could be to make two payments on a single debt each month. The first payment will only cover the interest you've accumulated that month. The second payment will completely be applied toward the principal. With this method, you get the part you must do out of the way and then get to see exactly how much of your debt you're paying off that month with the second payment. I find this can help when you start paying your bigger debts that feel like they never get smaller because you can see exactly how much you are paying on both interest and principal.

Can Debt Be Good?

I am a firm believer in using debt to your advantage, but it must be the right type of debt. Mortgages can fall into this category. If you live in an area where it costs more to rent than to own, having mortgage debt can be beneficial because it allows you to both save on rent and build equity without having to shell out all the money upfront. The same is true for investments.

As a real estate investor, if I were to fully fund all my investments with my own cash, I'd have to have a lot more capital than I do. Instead, I rely on banks or other investors to use their money, along with some of my own, to purchase properties. I then build that debt repayment into my projections for the project and make sure that I still make a profit. By spreading my money around to multiple investments, I can make more money in a shorter amount of time than if I were to buy one property in cash.

We will talk next about alternative income streams. If you find that you need to earn more money to pay your bills, reduce debt, and start investing, this will be the chapter for you.

CHAPTER 6
MAKING BANK

TLDR: The notion of being able to get rich quick is a fairytale. In reality, making money takes work, no matter how you do it.

I hate to say it but there's no such thing as getting rich quick, aside from winning the lottery or receiving a very large inheritance. Since neither of those are within reach for many of us, let's discuss ways you can increase your income. I'll warn you though, I don't like a lot of the ideas that are out there and personally won't recommend them.

I believe that making money takes work and the only person you can rely on to make that happen is yourself. Success doesn't just happen overnight and there are a lot of steps and hard work that goes into becoming successful. The key is to do the work, even when you don't see the payoffs right away. If you don't put that work in now, you won't be ready when an opportunity presents itself, and you won't grow your wealth.

My journey started with education. In my early twenties, I earned both a diploma in graphic design and an arts degree in sociology. Because of this combination, when I found a career in corporate communications, I was uniquely positioned to take advantage of the advancement opportunities that came my way. I had no formal training in communications, aside from a one-day seminar in business writing. But because I had a degree, even in a mostly unrelated field, I was able to work in a field I didn't even know existed.

I had loads of writing experience, thanks to my university days, and I had a significant understanding of layout and design from my diploma. This helped me when developing materials because I didn't have to use a designer and could save money and time – both important measurements in a corporate job.

I had also worked previously as an event planner, both as an employee and in my own business. In the communications world, you are often responsible for arranging press conferences, stakeholder presentations, tradeshow booths and workshops, fancy galas, and the list goes on. I had no idea that as an event planner, I was developing the skills I would need later in my career, but that's what happened, and they came in handy when I needed them.

It was a little serendipitous that the jobs and education I chose ended up providing me with the skills I would need to do a job I didn't even know existed. Throughout my twenties, when I was gaining all these skills, I was broke and didn't know where my life was going. I didn't yet know what career path I would take, and my decisions were based on the immediate future, rather than long-term planning. Looking back now, I can see that I was putting in the work that would pay off later – I just didn't know it yet.

Obviously, I'm a big proponent of education and I believe that whenever possible, we should strive to learn new skills. Depending on where you are in life, that could mean a degree or college course, or it could mean learning how to crochet or arrange flowers. Whatever the topic or level, so long as it's in something you're interested in and is worth the time and costs, you can't go wrong.

Is there something that you've been yearning to learn or that seems like it might be interesting? Do you have any capacity to learn new skills right now? If so, perhaps you can find a friend or online course that can give you an introduction to the topic, without having to invest a ton of time or money. Even baby steps can pay off if you're walking in the right direction.

Career Advancement

I didn't become successful overnight, and I didn't just magically have the money I needed to start my own businesses and grow my wealth. I needed a traditional job and career to do that. Despite my desire to leave the corporate world, I spent nearly a decade engrossed in it before I had the opportunity to leave.

I started my communications career through a temp agency. I had been job searching for months, both before and after our cross-country move, and was unsuccessful. My goal that inspired my decision to move my family was to land a government job in social policy. I thought I'd start by working with the temp agency to bring in some cash while I applied to the positions I really wanted.

The temp agency placed me in a communications role with a diamond mining company because of my degree and ability to write. The position was temporary, and the pay sucked but as it turned out, I was good at it. Before my term was up, an indeterminate role became available in the same company. I applied and even though I didn't have much experience, I got the job as a communications advisor.

Two years later, I was laid off. Instead of wallowing in self-pity, I found myself job hunting, like I had planned to do when I first started with the temp agency. I worked my network and landed a role as a senior advisor in government. I had taken something that could have been negative and instead got a higher-paying job with a better title and more responsibility. It wasn't social policy but as it happened, I liked this better.

A few years later, I spent some time considering what I really wanted at that stage of my life and decided to focus on making more money. I was recently separated and after years of spending much of my time volunteering and becoming a leader in my community, I was barely getting by. At that time, making money became my priority rather than career growth and so I returned to mining with a higher-paying job but a lower job title and less responsibility. I didn't have to leave my government job, but I knew I could grow my salary much faster in the private sector.

Over the next three years, I worked hard to grow professionally and move up through the ranks. In that time, I earned three promotions and increased my income by over a hundred thousand dollars per year. I didn't just wait for opportunities to fall into my lap. I went after them with determination. I sought out advancement opportunities and pitched new ones when they didn't yet exist.

Millennials, and women in particular, seem to believe that hard work will just pay off; and that our superiors will notice our determined effort to go above and beyond and promote us. That's usually not how it works. You must look for opportunities and market yourself as the person who will help fix whatever issues the company is facing. You need to be strategic with your career development and take chances, even when they seem a little far-fetched. Be intentional with your career because no one else will.

Using this mindset, over the nine years from when I first considered how to change my family's future, to the day I left the corporate world, I increased my income by 900%.

As it is for most people, having a traditional career was my most lucrative income stream. But it didn't have to be, and I certainly didn't want it to be that way forever. I was determined to find a way to leave the corporate world and still earn enough income each year to support my family in the lifestyle we wanted. I didn't want to go back to being poor, just so that I could be home with my kids more. I wanted both money and freedom. In other words, I wanted to have it all, or at least the Millennial version of having it all.

Thankfully for us, that doesn't have to mean a demanding career, unbalanced household duties, and childcare, taking on the mental load, staying fit, looking pretty, attending to all your partner and children's needs, looking after aging parents, taking care of yourself and having an active and fulfilling social life. That was for the Boomers and Generation X. For us, having it all can means that you spend your days the way you want and with the people you want. You take care of your responsibilities but without the burden of having to accomplish everything. Time can be our friend, rather than our foe. Sounds nice, doesn't it?

If increasing your income through education, promotions or career advancement doesn't seem to be in the cards for you, let's look at some other options for increasing your income.

Alternative Income Streams

An income stream is a way to make money. The idea is that money flows to you in one or more ways, like streams of water. Income streams can be passive, meaning you don't have to do much, if anything, and the money continues to flow. Or you might have to actively work to keep up the flow, in which case, it would be an active income stream. In the same way, income can come from a side hustle or a main gig. A side hustle is something you do in your free time and is usually part-time. It's in addition to your main job, also called your day job.

You will have to decide if any of these income streams will work for you. The amount of time and capital required will be a big factor, but so will your income goals and the skills you possess. Take some time to read through the income streams I highlight and pay close attention to the risk level, time commitment, and capital required. To make it easier, I've listed that information at the top of each section.

Starting from the more passive income streams, let's review some popular ways that folks are making money, whether as a side hustle or their main job. I'll share my experiences and my own opinions, but it's paramount that you evaluate what will work for you, based on your circumstances.

Traditional Investing

- Requires capital
- Mostly passive
- Mid-level risk

Traditional investing includes everything from buying individual stocks to putting money into a Registered Retirement Savings Plan (RRSP) account managed by a financial institution. We'll learn more specifically about investment accounts in later chapters, so don't get too caught up in the types of investments just yet.

To make money using investments, you will need capital, or money, to start. You can invest yourself using a discount online broker like Wealthsimple or Questrade, or through your bank's app or website. You can also hire someone to invest your money for you in a managed account like an RRSP.

Many people believe there's significant risk involved in traditional investing. While this can be true, some products allow you to virtually remove all risks and still earn investment income. There can also be tax advantages to investing, like earning tax-free interest or reducing your income tax obligations – something that isn't as easy with other investment types.

Personally, I have done well with traditional investing and have seen as much as fifty percent growth over one year. I make sure to have a diversified portfolio of self-directed stocks and ETFs, as well as GICs and managed retirement accounts (I'll explain all of this later).

Real Estate

- ❖ Requires capital
- ❖ Can be as passive or active as you want
- ❖ Some risk

Real estate investing is so diverse but probably as misunderstood as traditional investing. We've all heard horror stories about problem tenants or mismanaged properties. Like everything though, we usually only hear about the extremes of real estate investing because the millions of happy tenants and landlords don't have much to talk about.

Most people who invest in real estate make their money through rental income, asset appreciation or by renovating and reselling the property for a profit. I've increased my overall wealth by using all three of these strategies for different properties.

Rental income is earned when you purchase either a residential or commercial property and rent it to someone else for a fee. A residential property is where someone will live, like a house or apartment. A commercial property is a building, land, or other asset used by a business.

If the rent they pay you is more than your expenses for the property, you'll earn rental income. In the same way, if you have a mortgage for the property, part of the rent you receive will go towards paying the principal portion of the mortgage. This in turn reduces your liability on the property and increases your wealth. If the property increases in value, this is called asset appreciation, which also increases your wealth.

Personal Case Study:

I bought my first residential rental property, along with my partner, three years ago. The property was already rented to a couple, so we began earning rental income right away. The mortgage is fairly low, so after three years, we paid off some of the principal and earned back more than we originally invested through the down payment. We've also completed renovations on the property which has increased the value, should we choose to sell. To help illustrate, I've included the actual numbers (rounded for ease) below:

Purchase price	$130,000
Down payment and purchase fees	$30,000
Rental income after expenses (36 months)	$32,000
Renovations	$30,000
Current value	$250,000
Current principal owing to the bank	$82,000

Looking at the numbers above, we initially invested $30,000 of our own money to purchase this property. In the three years since, we've received $32,000 in rental income after expenses, which we have reinvested into the home in the form of renovations, with $2,000 left over.

Thanks to asset appreciation, the property is now valued at $250,000 with $82,000 left owing on the mortgage. Should we sell today, forgetting for a moment realtor fees and other variable costs involved in selling, we would have $168,000 left over. After reimbursing ourselves the initial $30,000 investment, the remaining $138,000 of asset appreciation, plus the additional $2,000 from rental income, would be our profit. That means that, should we sell this property today, we would have earned $140,000 in three years from an initial $30,000 investment.

We've all heard of the myriad of reality television series that focus on renovating houses for a profit. Thanks to the popularity of these shows and some extra downtime during the pandemic, many would-be house-flippers tried their hand at this recently. The federal government has tried to slow this trend, though I can't imagine why, through their residential property flipping rule. Now, if you were to flip a house within a 12-month period, your profits will be taxed as business income and no longer get special treatment as a capital gain.

Where I live, there are very few houses to either rent or buy. Supplies are expensive and available land is minimal. There are also many aging homes that should be updated. On one hand, there are grants from the federal government available to upgrade a residential home and make it more energy efficient. On the other hand, there are rules like the property flipping rule that penalize the companies that are trying to do just that. Yes, there is a profit involved, but at the end of the day, the house becomes safer, and more energy efficient and it will last longer than if left as is. The problem with how this is being handled is that it rewards only those folks who can purchase their own home and penalizes renters who are then left to live in the aging housing stock with landlords who will be taxed unfairly if they upgrade and can't access grants that others can.

While not completely passive, real estate investing can be as passive or as active as you'd like. My partner and I recently toured a residential property with the idea to renovate and resell it. This would be completely active and would be more like a job while we were renovating. On the other hand, we used to employ a property manager for one of our properties so other than the odd email, we didn't have to do anything, and the money would just show up in our account.

If you're interested in real estate income, but don't want to purchase a property or deal with tenants yourself, there are other options available to you. You can purchase stock in a Real

Estate Investment Trust (REIT), rent out a bedroom in your home, or offer short-term rentals when you are out of town. You could also rent out a parking spot or even storage space in your garage or on your lawn. The possibilities are endless, really. Just make sure you follow all local laws and regulations and that you make sure you are covered by insurance, should anything go wrong.

Of course, there's also some risk in real estate investing. Tenants may not pay their rent, leaving you with bills to pay and no cash flow to pay them. The real estate market could take a turn and your property may lose value. A fire could destroy the asset and depending on your insurance policy, you could be left paying to replace it. My partner and I have developed ways to reduce some of these risks and make real estate investing work for us. If you're interested in learning more about real estate investing, visit my website Cherishwinsor.com for more resources.

Selling Things You Create

- Requires minimal capital
- Active
- Can be done from home
- Flexible

In our connected world, there are a myriad of things you can create and sell for a profit. The upside is that you can often do this at home on your schedule. There are traditional goods like crafts (think things like jewelry, woodworking, vinyl designs, or crocheted items) or food that might be sold online or at a vendor market.

These can make you a profit, but they take a lot of time and require you to sell each item individually, so your potential revenue is limited. Of course, if you enjoy crafting or making things, by all means, sell them. There are just other ways to make a higher profit for similar efforts.

My ex-husband and I used to sell woodwork like cutting boards and wine holders. He worked at a wood shop at the time and would use his lunch hours to make our inventory using the tools there. I then sold the items at craft fairs and through our website. We didn't make much money, but he enjoyed the creativity that came with making beautiful pieces and he honed his skill.

Digital products are things like e-books, online courses, print-on-demand books and organizers. You can even create your own clothing line and sell it through an online retailer. Digital tools allow you to create an item once and sell it to many people. It's kind of like compound interest in that the same investment can grow exponentially over time.

We all have skills that we can use to create or sell products. The key is to figure out what you are good at and find a way to share it with the world. Are you particularly good at gardening? Perhaps you can share your method for growing the juiciest tomatoes through an e-book or short online course. If you don't possess the skills to write that book or develop that course, that's okay too. There are online websites like Fiverr where you can hire someone to do that part for you. They can take your knowledge and turn it into a product that you can then market and sell.

I dropped out of high school about halfway through grade 10 and got my GED when I was nineteen years old. At the time, all I had to do was pass four exams over two days showing that I had achieved an equivalent level of skill in the core subjects. Having missed almost all of high school, I barely passed my English writing exam. It's ironic that I then ended up excelling in a career in communications that meant my core skill was writing. Who would have thought?

Aside from my writing experience, I also have training and experience in building websites and digital design. This has allowed me to develop resources and products, just like this book, that can both help others and provide me with a small income.

Doing Things For Others Or Freelancing

- Requires minimal capital
- Active
- Can be done from home
- Flexible

Freelancing involves using your skills to provide a service to someone else through some form of contract. Freelance gigs are usually short-term but can be part-time or full-time. You can find these kinds of jobs through traditional job postings, or you can advertise your services and have folks come to you.

I mentioned in the last section that you can hire folks to ghostwrite an e-book for you or have someone put together a digital course based on your instructions. This category includes the people that would do that work for you. Other options include things like designing social media ads and managing social media pages for other businesses, providing bookkeeping services or writing business plans, house-sitting, or dog-walking. It could be almost anything you can think of. If you are having trouble coming up with ideas, I suggest you have a look through an online freelance marketplace like Fiverr, Upwork, or Freelancer.com

What separates this category from a regular job is the flexibility and creativity that these income streams can provide.

Overtime Or A Second Job

- No capital
- Active
- Likely out of the house
- Can lead to burnout

Some jobs offer the option of overtime, and this can be great when you need a little extra cash. It's tough to do this long term though and it can take away from your other responsibilities. Depending on your job and your family commitments; however, you may feel that an extra shift every week or two is doable and that might be a good balance while you are paying down debt, building capital for your investments, or working on a plan for another income stream.

If your job doesn't offer overtime, or you want something different than what you do all day but still need that extra cash, a second job may be right for you. This could be a service job in a restaurant or bar, or it could mean driving for a delivery service. I've known people who drive for Amazon or DoorDash regularly. I've also known people who drive a taxi or school bus, work in a garden shop during the summer, pick up occasional shifts at a prison, or wait tables.

I personally have never had a second job, mostly because I've been raising children since I was eighteen and there wasn't time or childcare. When I needed to make extra money, I've instead focused on advancing in my career or freelancing.

Offer Childcare

- Requires some capital
- Active
- Significant regulations

If your children are young, offering childcare in your home may be a good income stream for you. Keep in mind that there are regulations about the number of children you can provide care for, that are not your own. If this is something you would like to pursue, check with your local childcare authority to find out the rules where you live.

Years ago, while running my event planning businesses and looking after my other young children, I watched my nephews while their mom worked. I worked from home anyway and had my own kids, so it was a win-win for both families. My kids got to socialize, I made a little extra cash and their mom got to work knowing her kids were looked after.

When my daughter was about fourteen months old and I took my first mining job, childcare spots were scarce. Through an online search, I found a mom with three kids who was willing to look after her for a very reasonable rate. That mom was looking for a way to make extra money with two kids in school and a young one around the same age as my daughter. From that time, until she started school, my daughter spent most weekdays with her and I'm grateful for the care she received.

Start a Business

- Likely requires significant capital
- Very active
- Potential for growth and flexibility

If you can dream it, you can turn it into a business. But that doesn't mean you should. Starting and managing your own business can be a great option but it takes a significant amount of work to get a new business to a point that it is sustainable.

I've mentioned several businesses that I have started over the years. Some were lucrative and some were definitely not. Each one was created at a different point in my life and for a different purpose. I'll give you a few examples:

My event planning business was created as part of a program offered to Employment Insurance (EI) recipients. I had been laid off from my job and while receiving EI, I learned of a program that would continue to provide me with a small income for up to a year while I developed a business. This model allowed for less of a financial burden during the crucial first year of my business and since I hadn't found another job, I decided to offer event planning services geared towards children's events. In the end, the businesses didn't survive past that first year, but I was able to walk away without any debt because of the program.

More recently, I was asked to return as a temporary employee to a company I had previously worked for because they needed help with a specific project. I already had a full-time job so I countered their offer with a proposal to freelance the work, mostly during evenings and weekends. Once they agreed and I cleared it with my employer, I created a business that would provide the services to this company. Once the contract was finished, I picked up a few more but eventually decided not to renew my business licence.

When starting a business, you need to consider all aspects. Just because you're good at making designer cakes, it doesn't mean that a business selling them would be feasible. There are just so many other tasks that go along with operating a business that owners often end up ignoring their duties or getting too burnt out early on.

I currently own multiple businesses, one of which is in its second year and has yet to make a profit any month. We've maxed out the amount of personal capital we would like to contribute to the business, but it still isn't able to maintain itself from month to month. This is a failing business and one that should probably have been closed months ago. We've developed a plan to try to increase revenue and decrease expenses so that we minimize our loss but will likely have to decide eventually to close it.

After all of that, you may wonder why I'd even bring up the possibility of starting your own business. Well, for some people it can be a good option. As I said, you just need to exercise caution. If this is a path you want to take, please take the time to read business books. If you head to my website

Cherishwinsor.com, I recommend a couple that may be of help to you.

Affiliate Marketing

- Active
- Flexible
- Requires a large audience or time commitment to build one

Affiliate marketers drive traffic to a specific website and get paid to do it. Have you ever noticed a blogger or Tiktokker who shares their "favourite" products and provides you a link to buy them yourself? They're earning money each time someone clicks on that link or buys that product. Like hiring someone to advertise the product or service, the company hires someone to promote it, but usually in their own way and to their audience.

Affiliate marketers can run ads themselves or send out emails to their email lists; they can use social media to share with their friends, family, or followers. They can also write articles or design courses with affiliate links embedded. The possibilities are pretty much only hindered by your imagination.

I've personally never tried this method as it seems like it would be a lot of work with little reward. I don't have a large online audience and don't have the desire to make one. If this is something that you're interested in, I encourage you to do your research and fully understand the process first.

Multi-level Marketing

Avon, Tupperware, Mary-Kay, Younique – these are all well-known examples of brands that use the multi-level marketing (MLM) model to sell their products. These businesses rely on the recruitment and participation of people who also sell their product for them. The product could be makeup, candles, leggings, kitchen gadgets, or anything else. This business model, while legal, preys on people who are looking for an income and often need flexibility (translation: moms). If you don't believe me, consider the types of things that are sold through this business model. Most of them are items that are more often bought by women.

With so many moms looking for ways to earn an income while looking after their children, these businesses seem like a great option. They are products that moms use and that can be talked about and shared with the seller's friends and family. These initial conversations lead to their first sales and the business model appears to work.

Often, these folks do very well at first, but then sales begin to taper off once they've already sold to everyone in their social circle. MLM companies are smart though and designed another way to continue to make money once their sellers reach this stage.

Not only do these women sell the product, but they also recruit other people to sell it. Then, because the first seller recruited those new people, the first seller gets a cut of the profit. This cycle continues until everyone in their social circle has had the opportunity to buy or join the company as a seller. But then what? At this point, the seller has already been touting the glorious merits of the product for so long and likely invested so much of their own money, that it's hard to leave it behind.

Have you ever noticed or been approached by a multi-level marketer? They're often so convinced of the merits of the product that they're shouting about it from the rooftops. Then, after a few months, things get quieter, and before long, they don't talk about it anymore. The posts have disappeared from their social media, and they stop trying to recruit you.

Those who get involved in this model rarely stay with the company for very long. Some will hop to a new MLM company, but many will be left with unsold products and potentially more debt than they started with. They worked hard and felt like they were building something but, in the end, only helped the company they worked for. Now I know this isn't true for everyone and some people can be a little successful with this model, but it will never be a true wealth generator.

While this was just the tip of the iceberg when it comes to income streams, I hope this chapter was helpful and that you were able to spend some time considering what might work for you. Whatever you decide, be sure to do your research and look for resources that are specific to Canada and your own jurisdiction. Laws and regulations can vary significantly even between cities so make sure you're aware of them.

CHAPTER 7
PERSONAL FINANCE ISN'T HARD

TLDR: You can understand personal finances and achieve financial freedom. Canadians have access to accounts that can help them save for their kid's education, buy a house, retire, or just increase their wealth. Investments live inside of accounts.

Personal finance seems scary to many, simply because we weren't properly taught about it and the professionals make it seem complicated. Let me tell you, that's by design. A traditional investment broker is there to make money. They do not exist to help you make money; they exist to make money for themselves and their employers. Banks are akin to giant corporations. Everyone is out to make money for themselves, regardless of how they sell it. This is a key lesson in your financial journey.

I find it helpful to think of investment tools sold by banks as products. Just like buying a pool noodle from Walmart, everything they offer you is a product they're trying to sell you, and vis-à-vis from which they will make money. Banks and others in the financial industry make finance seem complicated so that they can sell you their expertise and, in turn, take your money from you. But that's not right. You can understand personal finance and what it means to do well, even if you've never heard of a GIC or know what an asset class is.

Now sit back and let me spill the tea on the basics of the Canadian personal finance world. By the end of this chapter, I'll have you feeling like a financial guru, and you'll wonder why you ever believed that BS from the so-called experts.

As Canadians, we're used to most of our literature, TV, movies, or digital content coming from the U.S. In a lot of ways, this doesn't matter, but when it comes to personal finance, it's important to make sure you're learning from Canadian sources. While some of the very basics are the same, our systems and products vary greatly, as do the rules, laws, and tax implications associated with them. This book uses data and examples from Canada and is best-suited for individuals living in Canada.

Moreso than the U.S., Canada's banking system is heavily regulated, which is why we have much fewer banking options than our neighbours to the south. Have you ever noticed how many airlines there are in the States? Well, their banks are kind of the same. There are so many. Here in Canada, we have the big five – Royal Bank (RBC), The Bank of Montreal (BMO), Canadian Imperial Bank of Commerce (CIBC), The Bank of Nova Scotia (Scotia), and Toronto-Dominion Bank (TD). There are also credit unions and some smaller banks.

More recently, we're starting to see an increase in online banking options for Canadians like Equitable Bank (EQ), Tangerine, or Simplii. These banks offer online-only services, no or lower fees, and often provide better interest rates, though that isn't always the case. Regardless of the type, all Canadian banks are federally regulated and are obligated to follow rules that are designed to protect your money and investments.

Investment Accounts

Canadians have the potential to save for life events using more than just regular savings accounts. When saving for retirement, you can choose from a Registered Retirement Savings Plan (RRSP), Locked-In Retirement Account (LIRA), or even a Tax-free Savings Account (TFSA). Your child's education can be funded by a Registered Education Savings Plan (RESP). You can use a First Home Savings Account (FHSA) to save for a home downpayment or borrow a portion of your non-locked-in RRSP.

We'll get more into these and the differences between them below. The important thing to remember is that all of these are *accounts* and are not investments themselves. Think of them as the container where you put your money. In the illustration below, the accounts would be the filing cabinet drawers. These will not guarantee that your money will grow. For that, you will need to assign your money to an investment or asset class, like the file folders below. As you read through this section, feel free to refer back to this graphic if things get confusing.

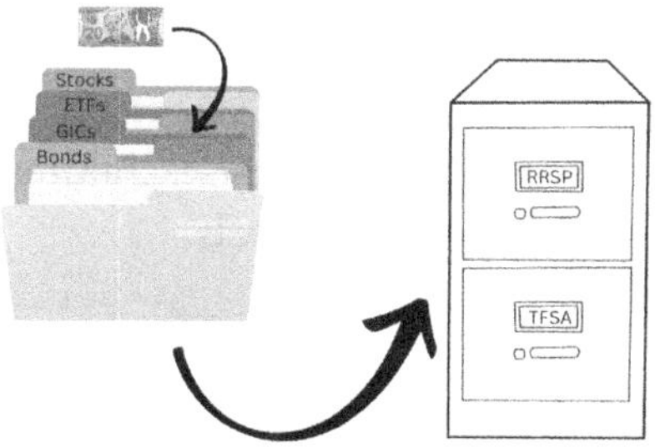

Retirement Accounts

RRSP

An RRSP is just what its name implies: a savings plan for retirement that's registered with the federal government. While it is considered a plan, it's helpful to think of it more like an account. You can open an RRSP with a traditional bank, online bank, credit union, or insurance company at any time and you can have more than one.

The advantage of putting your retirement savings into an RRSP is that it can reduce the amount of income tax that you must pay each year. As you earn income and file taxes, the federal government will determine your RRSP deduction limit each year. While you can contribute any amount up to your deduction limit, you'll get the full advantage of reduced taxes if you deposit your full deduction limit amount.

Then, at retirement, you withdraw your savings, plus any interest earned, and pay taxes at that time. Many of us plan to have less income in retirement and RRSPs allow you to defer paying taxes until that time. This in turn reduces your overall taxes paid because your tax bracket will likely be lower as you age.

RRSPs can be managed through your financial institution, which means they invest the money on your behalf, for a fee. You can also choose to manage your savings yourself through a self-directed RRSP. If you have a spouse or common-law partner, you can also set up an RRSP for them. This is helpful if one of you takes time off to raise children or if there's a large difference in your income levels.

RRSP deductions are a little funny in that the amount you include is calculated beginning in March each year until the end of February the following year, rather than following a calendar year. This allows you to see how much income you earned during the previous tax year, and then contribute additional money to your RRSP, if necessary, to get the full advantage of the tax deferral.

While the tax advantages can be great, you want to make sure that any money you put into an RRSP is money that you're okay leaving there for a long time. There are only three situations when you may consider withdrawing from an RRSP: when buying your first house, paying for your own or your spouse's education, or upon retirement. Withdrawals to buy a home or education must be paid back within ten years or you will be taxed on the withdrawal as income.

Keep in mind that some RRSPs are locked in, which means you cannot withdraw funds, even for buying a house or funding your education. Typically, locked in RRSPs are the result of an employer-offered retirement savings plan.

When I left my first mining job, I was two days away from the threshold to lock in my retirement account. This worked out well for me because I was able to transfer the funds from my employer's retirement plan into a personal RRSP, and then withdraw $25,000 for the purchase of my first home. Had I been employed with that company two days longer, the account would have become locked in, and I wouldn't have been able to buy my home when I did. The amount that you can withdraw as part of the Home Buyers Plan has since increased to $35,000.

LIRA

If you have a pension plan with your employer, you may wonder what happens to it if you leave before retirement. Most likely, your money will be moved to a LIRA. Like an RRSP, a LIRA is tax-sheltered, which means you don't pay tax until you withdraw. These accounts are registered with the federal government and are locked in, meaning you cannot take any money out before retirement, except for in very specific circumstances like reduced life expectancy.

LIRAs are also used in the case of divorce when a pension is divided between the spouses.

Other Accounts

RESP

RESPs allow you to save for your children's education and can be used for trade schools, college, or university. These accounts can be opened once your child has a Social Insurance Number. Depending on the amount you save each year and your family income, your children can receive additional funding in their RESPs from the federal government. Both the Canada Learning Bond and the Canada Education Savings Grant can provide thousands of extra dollars toward your child's education.

You don't receive a tax deduction for contributing to an RESP. Your child will be taxed when they make a withdrawal but because students generally have very low income, they don't usually end up paying any taxes.

RESPs can be opened for individual children or as part of a family plan. Some allow you to contribute money whenever you like, and others require monthly contributions. Like RRSPs, most financial institutions provide them, but I caution you to do your research before making your selection.

My first foray into investing was when I was still in university. I was twenty-three with three young kids. Being in university myself, I was very aware of how expensive it would be to educate my kids and I didn't want them to incur the same kind of debt I had accumulated.

I came across a company that offered RESPs and I set up a meeting. I even went so far as to set up a presentation by a representative of the company to other student parents. Everything about the idea of investing in my kids' education made sense and I was able to pick either an investing model that allowed automatic withdrawals from my chequing account or an ad-hoc model where I invested birthday or extra money, and other family members could also contribute. I chose the latter and signed up all my kids.

What I didn't understand was that the company I had chosen had so many hidden fees that after a year of investing, my kids' RESP accounts were practically empty. I was so disheartened that I gave up on investing for a very long time.

If I knew then what I know now, I would have opened a self-directed RESP for each of my children and managed them myself. That way, I wouldn't have lost my hard-earned money to fees and my children would be better set for post-secondary now. But since I was burned that first time, I never did try again and lost out on all the extra money the government would have contributed.

FHSA

Like using an RRSP to purchase your first home, the federal government now offers a savings account for specifically this purpose. If you haven't yet purchased a home, you can open an FHSA through a financial institution to begin saving for a down payment on your primary residence. As with RRSPs, you can choose either a managed or self-directed account.

Contributions to your FHSA are tax deductible, with a maximum contribution of $8,000 per year and a lifetime total of $40,000. What's more, your growth is not considered income and therefore not taxed. Even better, unlike RRSPs, FHSAs are not taxable when withdrawn, if you meet all of the criteria. If you're looking for a way to reduce your taxes and save for a home, this could be a win-win.

TFSA

Now, all the account types we've discussed so far are for specific purposes – retirement, education or buying a home. This next one is a Tax-Free Savings Account, and it can be used for anything. You do not need a specific purpose, which if you remember, is the key to building wealth.

Each year, the federal government sets a maximum TFSA contribution limit for all Canadians over eighteen. In 2024, that limit is $7,000. Since introduced in 2009, the cumulative limit for all years is $95,000. That means that if you were at least 18 years old in 2009, which includes about half of all Millennials, you can contribute up to the maximum amount.

For those younger Millennials among us, your total will be reduced by the maximum limit each year until you turned 18. The easiest way to check your contribution room if you've never contributed to a TFSA is on the Canada Revenue Agency website.

Unlike the other accounts we've discussed, TFSAs do not reduce the amount of tax you pay on your income. A TFSA is an after-tax savings account. However, the power of a TFSA is that it allows you to earn interest or dividends, without having to pay tax on that growth.

Unfortunately, many people don't understand how TFSAs work and they treat them like a simple savings account, never investing the money and in turn, never really seeing any rewards. Without a tax break on your contribution and very little growth, why do these folks even bother? Likely because they don't know any better.

To get the maximum advantage of this great tool, you need to take things a step further and invest your money into an asset. That asset could be stocks, something many people are familiar with, or it could be a GIC, ETF, mutual fund, or other similar investments.

Of course, you can invest in these assets without using a TFSA, but then the money you earn will be taxable. You need the advantage of the TFSA umbrella to reap the most rewards.

Asset Classes

In personal finance, asset classes are how we group similar types of investments. Some of the most common in Canada are equities, fixed income, and cash. There are also alternative investment types like real estate, cryptocurrency, and commodities. These terms can make asset classes seem complex but they're not really that complicated. We will discuss the first two below. We've already discussed HISAs, which are considered a cash investment. Other cash investments include the money you keep in a regular bank account, Guaranteed Investment Certificates (GICs), and money market funds. We'll talk more about those a little later in the chapter.

Equities or Stocks

The stock market is probably the most known and yet most scary investment vehicle for Canadian Millennials. We're familiar with the concept of buying and selling stocks, but we don't necessarily know how. Us older Millennials remember Will Smith's film *The Pursuit of Happiness* and the rags to riches story that it was based on. We conceptually understand that there's money to be made if you know what you're doing, but we also know that there's money to be lost and we're scared to try. After all, we've been conditioned our whole lives to believe the stock market is complicated and only professionals can reduce the risk of losing your hard-earned money. I call BS. No one, and I mean no one, can predict the stock market.

A few months ago, my partner and I had a lovely meal in the very first stock exchange building, located in Amsterdam, Netherlands. We were at the beginning of a month-long tour through seven European countries (retirement perk!) and happened upon this fabulous building. We sat at the back of the now-restaurant and read about the history of the stock exchange. I could visualize the men coming in through the main doors to start their trading of the day – over 400 years ago! Without meaning to, we wound up visiting other stock exchange buildings on that trip, but the history of this one was a treat.

Of course, the New York Stock Exchange is probably much more known by Canadians than the European versions. Canada also has its own called the Toronto Stock Exchange (TSX). This is where Canadian stocks are bought and sold.

While I'll use the word stock in its colloquial way, at its most basic, the word stock refers to a share in the ownership of a publicly traded company. Not to remind you of your Grade 4 English class but *share* is a noun; it's the item you buy, while stock is your part of the ownership in the company. Today, the words are mostly used interchangeably. Now with that little history and English lesson out of the way, let's get into what matters – buying or selling stock as a means by which to increase your wealth.

Buying stock has never been easier. In Canada, we have multiple online investment services that allow you to transfer funds from your Canadian bank account using just your phone. All you have to do is open an investment account, transfer funds into the account, then select a company to invest in.

Unlike a traditional investment broker, an online investment service might offer stock trading with zero or low commission when you choose your own stocks. They also usually offer lower fees than traditional services if you prefer that someone else manage your investments and make those choices for you.

But say you want to try your hand at managing your own stocks; how do you choose which ones to invest in? Well, that really depends on you. I've bought and sold stocks from various industries, holding them for different amounts of time and seeing varying degrees of success – and failure.

Are you looking for a long-term investment, something to hold on to for many years or do you think you would like the excitement of trying to time your purchases to get the best deal? Are you using money that you will need for something soon (not a great idea) or are you trying to build your wealth? Do you have the time and temperament to research individual companies and their stock or are you a fly-by-the-seat-of-your-pants type of girl? Do you want a stock that pays dividends or are you primarily interested in growth? I'm a little bit of all of this.

I think the first stock I purchased was Canadian Tire or Loblaws. I wanted a Canadian retail stock and these companies had been around for a long time. They did fairly well through the pandemic and when looking over the previous five years, I could see their potential growth. No one was writing about the merits of these stocks at the time, but they were both companies I was familiar with, and felt comfortable with their longevity. I've since sold my Loblaws stock, and my Canadian Tire has been down more than ten percent for months.

Another early stock I purchased was in one of the Big Five banks. Investment gurus usually recommend having stock in the financial industry long-term and I figured I couldn't go wrong. Almost immediately, that stock dropped and stayed low for nearly a year. Someone else I know purchased stock in another of the big five and had a similar experience.

My biggest risk was in a company that offered personal loans. It wasn't quite a predatory loan company, but it offered personal loans with higher interest rates than most banks. This was just as the pandemic was ending and interest rates began to climb. There were no articles that even mentioned this stock but given what I saw happening in the world around me, I thought it might be a good time to invest. I still own that stock and it has been one of my best performers.

Last year, I took the plunge and purchased some stock in Shopify. Other than a pandemic peak and fall, it has been doing well for a while. I read about the merits of this one, but I thought, well how can it go any higher? It was a stock to watch, and many people had already done well investing in it. I started relatively small because I thought there was a good chance it would fall again. Within a couple of months, it started to really climb, and I've seen growth of nearly fifty percent at times.

Whatever your style, make sure you do your research and don't just follow the masses. Sometimes, the experts are right and sometimes they are just plain wrong. What works for your friend may not work for you. It's important to diversify which means making sure you invest in different sectors and industries. Also, while stocks act very similarly in Canada and the U.S., when choosing stocks, you need to consider whether they're Canadian, U.S., or international stocks as they are all treated differently come tax time.

Fixed Income or Bonds

A bond is like a loan to the government or a corporation. Unlike a stock, you don't own a portion of the company when you purchase a bond. Instead, your bond will pay set interest over time, usually paid out twice per year. Then, when your bond reaches its end date, called maturity, it's paid out at face value.

Bonds are less risky than stocks, but they require a time commitment. Should you wish to sell your bond before it matures (the date you agreed to get your money back), you could face additional fees. I've never purchased a bond, so my knowledge is limited to what I've read.

Investments in Mixed Asset Classes

Some investment types allow you to invest in multiple securities, through a single investment. Think of it like a basket. Someone has a basket that they fill with all kinds of securities, like stocks and bonds. Then you invest in that basket, rather than each individual item inside.

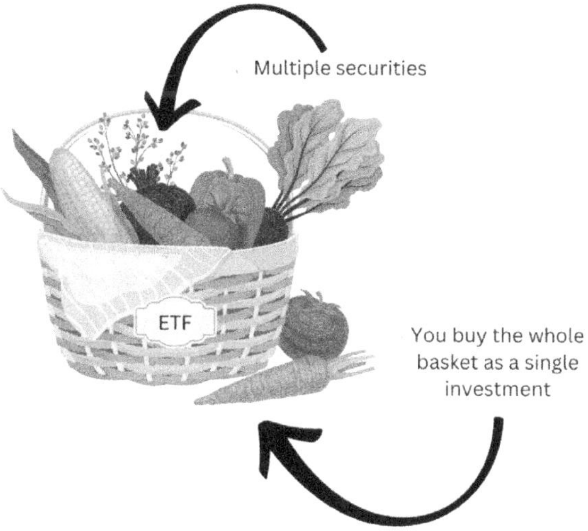

Exchange Traded Fund (ETF)

Similar to stocks, an ETF is bought and sold on an exchange. While a stock represents partial ownership in a single company, an ETF is a bundle of assets or securities. When you purchase an ETF, you're purchasing a portion of the fund, rather than a portion of the companies within that fund. ETFs are managed so there are fees involved, though they're usually quite small. The advantage of an ETF however is that you're diversifying your investment by sharing the risk between multiple companies, which usually results in less volatile swings as can be seen in single stocks.

I know this sounds a little more complicated, but I promise buying and selling ETFs can be simple and pain-free. They're even available through the same online investment services as stocks. Again, all you need to do is open an investment account, transfer funds into it, and select which ETF to purchase.

I own some ETFs, and while I find their value doesn't change much, I do receive dividends, which I invest back into the same ETFs or stocks.

Mutual Funds

A mutual fund is kind of like a cousin of an ETF because both offer a bundle of assets. The difference lies in how they're purchased and managed. While ETFs are bought and sold like stocks, mutual funds can only be purchased at the end of the trading day. The price of a mutual fund is also a little more complicated and based on its net asset value, rather than the simple supply and demand that forms the basis of stock pricing.

Many mutual funds are actively managed by a fund manager who decides what to buy and sell within the mutual fund to try to beat the market. But remember what I said before? No one can predict the market and the performance of mutual funds compared to the stock market can vary widely. When you add in the fees associated with a managed investment like a mutual fund, I prefer plain old stocks or ETFs. But that's just me. If mutual funds interest you, I encourage you to investigate them further.

Cash

When considering investments, we don't readily think of cash. But that's a mistake. Cash or cash equivalents can play an important role in your investment strategy. Cash investments offer more security than some of the other asset classes we've discussed, and they can be easier to access (called liquidity).

GICs

A GIC is a secure investment that can be purchased easily through any bank, credit union, or online discount broker. When purchasing, you agree to both the length of time you'll leave your money in the investment as well as the interest you will receive. This way, you know exactly how much you will earn on your investment. Just be careful not to withdraw your money before the agreed term is complete or you will pay penalties.

With higher interest rates thanks to the COVID-19 pandemic, GICs are becoming more popular because they offer guaranteed returns at higher rates than they did pre-pandemic. Just like a HISA, the posted interest rate is annual which means that you only receive the full posted rate, if you select a minimum commitment of one year.

For example, if you take out a GIC with a 5% interest rate and a length of 6 months, you'll only gain 2.5% in interest because you only held that GIC for half a year. Likewise, if you take out a 2-year GIC at 4%, you will earn 8%, 4 from the first year and 4 from the second.

Unlike bonds, GICs are eligible for insurance if you buy them through an insured institution, making them even more secure.

Whew, that was a lot, wasn't it? If you were unfamiliar with investment accounts and asset classes before reading this chapter, it can all seem a little overwhelming. Hopefully, my very brief intro helped, but if there was anything that piqued your interest, I encourage you to read more about it on the Canadian government website. Rules can change and it's always best to go to the source, rather than listening to someone's interpretation of the information.

SECTION

Three

YOUR PATH TO FINANCIAL FREEDOM

CHAPTER 8
EMBRACING FEAR AND DOING HARD THINGS

TLDR: Plan to succeed but prepare to fail. An ordinary life is lived by standing still. An extraordinary life is lived outside of your comfort zone.

Years ago, I worked in social research and one of the things we wanted to understand was how participating in a study affected those who were doing the research and those who were telling us their stories. Did the act of sharing your life story with someone affect you in any way? Did hearing others' sometimes very tragic stories impact the researcher? Was the act of sharing knowledge, called knowledge mobilization, a form of knowledge in itself?

During the years I worked on this study, I learned that the process of doing something can be just as worthwhile, if not more so, than the outcome. The act itself becomes the purpose.

When I ran for public office, I spent months mentally preparing myself for the potential of failure. I didn't plan on failing, but I knew that as a human who was afraid of public failure, I had some work to do to prepare.

I knew I could be successful as a politician if I won. I also knew that I could do a good job with my campaign. But, if I were to lose, I didn't think I could walk back into my regular job or face my friends. So, I worked on it. I read books and listened to podcasts. I took classes and spent time visualizing both winning and losing. I talked to friends and family, and I journaled.

In the end, I decided that the act of pushing myself so far outside of my comfort zone and trying for this giant thing was worth the potential embarrassment I might feel down the line. On the night the results came in, I was in a restaurant with my partner, kids, and campaign team members, along with a few other candidates from other ridings and media. As we watched the numbers come in on the screen, there was a moment where it became very clear that I wasn't going to win or even be in the top three.

I remember saying to my partner, "I just don't want to be last". I had dealt with the potential to fail but I hadn't considered that out of 6 candidates, I could come out last. But that's what happened. By 2 votes, I came in last place. I was devastated; I had failed, spectacularly. I went home and cried.

But then, I picked myself up and the next day, I went into my plan for failure. I sent messages to the other candidates. I congratulated those who had won. I thanked my team, and I took down all my signs. It was a blow to my ego, but I also had work to do – public work. I couldn't hide in my house like I wanted to.

Because I had put the time in and prepared myself for a potential failure, I knew that I could handle whatever came next. I didn't have to make decisions while feeling emotional or dwell on the failure. Instead, I could just put my plan into action. But guess what? By doing those tasks, I was slowly showing myself that I was okay. By writing a heartfelt congratulatory letter to the candidate who won, I focused on the future of our territory and our friendship. When I thanked my team, I reflected on the support I received. There were so many positives that came out of the experience, I just needed to look for them.

Now, four years later, I'm glad I tried. I grew professionally and personally in those few months, and I got a chance to see a side of myself I didn't always show. I hadn't lost anything from the experience (other than a bit of cash) and instead, I faced my fear of failure and survived. Because of the time I spent visualizing myself walking back into my place of employment or answering all the questions from friends or strangers, when I had to do it, it wasn't all that hard.

What scares me may not scare you and vice versa. My path is also not your path. When you dreamed of your Why and started to think about how you could achieve it, I'm sure you had ideas or dreams that scared you. The question I'll ask you is why? Why is it that so many of our dreams involve taking actions that scare us?

The answer is that fear has its place. We experience fear simply to keep us safe. As babies, we learn to fear things that could harm us, and this continues throughout our lives. When we consider radically changing our lives or doing things that are very different from our day-to-day, we often experience fear because our brains are considering the potential for danger. If we haven't done it before, how can we know if it could hurt us?

This is also true if we think something has the potential to harm us physically or otherwise. We can experience fear about something if we think it would be detrimental to our mental health, finances, relationships, or well-being. Whether because you've heard horror stories or haven't gathered enough information, if you believe something could be negative, you're more likely to fear it. I'll give you an example:

Have you ever considered purchasing an investment rental property and becoming a landlord? This is something I heard about when I was in my early 20s and considered for well over a decade before taking the leap. I had heard stories about people not paying their rent or damaging the property so extensively that the landlord lost thousands of dollars. I heard of problem tenants and difficult laws that didn't allow evictions, even when the landlord couldn't afford to carry the mortgage themselves. It all seemed a little scary because there was a potential for financial loss as well as disruptions to my well-being.

My natural response was to fear the potential financial and mental impact, but this was at odds with my Why and the path I wanted to use to get there. If I had let that fear win, I wouldn't be retired today. I would also have a much lower net worth and would experience more stress day-to-day by continuing to work my demanding job. The things I feared, less financial well-being and stress, would have happened by doing nothing!

One of the biggest lessons I can impart and that I hope you take from this book is to trust your gut and take those leaps of faith. DO NOT let fear ever stand in your way. We've all failed at times, but I'm sure you have succeeded so many more times.

You can't get anywhere if you stay still and if you want to achieve your goals, you're going to have to do scary or hard things. One of the keys to achieving your dreams and realizing your Why is to plan for success but prepare for failure.

Now, let's walk through the steps I use to overcome fear and walk confidently towards my future. If you're up for it, go ahead and try it out on one of the paths you're considering.

Step one – Identify your fear

Take a moment to think about something you want to achieve and try to identify what scares you about it. If you need a little prompt, think back to your Why from the first chapter and identify a path you might take to get there. A few years ago, my Why was financial freedom for myself and my kids. One of the paths I wanted to take to get there was rental income from investment properties. This semi-passive income stream seemed to be an ideal fit for someone interested in real estate, who wasn't afraid to get their hands dirty and wanted to retire early. The fears I had about this unknown path were financial ruin and the potential stress of problem tenants.

Step two – Identify the root of your fear

Once I've identified the specific fear, I find it helpful to identify what could happen if my fears were to be realised, because that's where the fear is coming from. Continuing with the rental example, here are some of the worst potential outcomes for me:

- I would not only lose everything I invested into the property but could also be liable for an injury or damages to another property.
- I wouldn't be able to afford to make the necessary payments (mortgage, insurance, property tax, utilities) if the tenants didn't pay their rent. This would in turn cause me to default and ruin my credit.
- I would spend so much time and effort dealing with maintenance or tenant issues that I would be forced to give up the property without making any money from it.
- The housing market would crash, and I would be upside down on my investment, meaning I owed more than it was worth.

These are all very scary and yet possible outcomes. Which is why most people don't get any further than this step. They let their fear of the worst possible outcome stand in their way. They don't realise that by working through a few more easy steps, they would be in a much better position to make a wise decision that isn't based solely on fear.

For you, consider what aspect of your dream you are most afraid of and what the worst possible outcomes could be. You may be tempted to write something like financial ruin as a potential outcome, but I encourage you to be more specific, like in the examples above. Exactly how could this dream of yours fail and what would that potentially mean for you?

Step three – Educate yourself and prepare

In reality, our fear will keep us from making some terrible mistakes but not because we're too scared to try. In fact, our fear acts as a warning so that we can then take the time to do the work we need to properly consider potential outcomes and mitigate any issues.

For each of the worst-case scenarios you identified, consider whether there's anything you can do to reduce the potential of a negative outcome. Could you learn more about the topic or speak to someone who has been through a similar situation and is now on the other side of it? Are there steps you can take to reduce the potential of any of those scenarios or eliminate them altogether?

Instead of worrying about being liable for injury or damage, I could get insurance. By properly considering the math, and making sure my cash flow was sufficient, I could be sure I'd be able to afford disruptions. Instead of spending my time dealing with issues, I could hire a property manager and include the costs in my affordability calculations. I could educate myself on local real estate trends and make an informed decision on the property I bought and at what price. Of all the worst possible outcomes, there was something I could do to mitigate the potential negative impact.

It's important that for whatever you do, you don't just charge headfirst into the unknown without doing the prep work. So, when we experience fear, it's a good reminder that we need to do more work.

Step four - Visualize and practice relaxation

With the concrete work out of the way, it's time to motivate yourself by using techniques that often go together with mindfulness. By now, you've worked your way through the potential negative impacts of your dream and found ways to mitigate them. Even still, I bet your fear is still alive and well. That's because we are emotional creatures, and we can't just persuade our minds to release our fears with facts. Most of us need a little more than that.

It may feel a little funny at first but with practice, it'll get easier. When you've got a few uninterrupted moments, I want you to find a comfortable spot to sit. When you're ready, lower your shoulders so that they are relaxed. Breathe deeply. Take your time and continue to focus on your breathing until you feel yourself relax.

Now, think of your Why and the path you want to take to get there. Imagine yourself having already achieved it. Try to focus on how you feel or how others feel around you. Focus on the details. If you get stuck on your fears, let them come and then let them go. Don't dwell but also don't try to push them away. Try to stay relaxed through the emotions that come up as you consider your fears.

Once you've done this exercise a few times, try switching it up and consider what it might be like if you try and don't succeed. As you work through the scenario, try to identify the emotions you're feeling and sit with them. Rather than worst-case scenarios, consider instead a likely outcome, then continue until you identify a path forward.

When I was preparing to start my political campaign, I would do this exercise often. Because my fear was social and focused on how others would view my failure, I visualized myself having to face the people in my life. I would see myself running into someone at the grocery store and having to talk about the loss.

I thought about returning to work and having colleagues stop by my office with pitying looks. It was uncomfortable but I pushed myself to do it.

Then, when I did lose the election and lived those experiences, I knew how to handle them. I had visualized myself congratulating the winner, then in reality, I took the time to write personal notes to my fellow candidates and made a point to be out in public. I knew what I would say to people when they asked about the campaign. I worked for the government at the time, so my office was very politically involved, and this was my biggest hurdle. When it came time to return to work, I was able to do so because I had worked through the outcome and identified a path forward. By the time I returned to work, I knew I was planning to leave that job and so I saw it as a chance to finish up some projects and say goodbye, rather than a step backward.

Step five - Flip the script and revise negative self-talk

This one is a little out there, but I encourage you to try it and have a little fun while you're at it. Own that fear! Say to yourself, "I am afraid of _______ and I'm going to do it anyway. The experience is worth the outcome, whatever it is." Say it out loud. Shout it if you want. Repeat this, or a version of it to yourself, whenever the doubt and fear creep up.

When You Fail

Sometimes you are going to fail, just like I did with my short-lived political career, and that's completely okay. You're going to be okay. Failure is a part of trying and if you've done the work, you'll already have a plan on how to handle the failure. Then, once you're on the other side, you can take stock and decide on a new path or way forward. Your Why is important to you so don't let fear be the reason you don't achieve it.

CHAPTER 9
WHAT'S NEXT?

TLDR: Thrive, don't just survive.

The title of this book is based on a famous quote from Maya Angelou. The author, poet, and civil activist, said, "My mission in life is not merely to survive, but to thrive; and to do so with some passion, some compassion, some humor, and some style."

Surviving is not thriving. Many of us Millennials are just surviving life. We're burnt out trying to do and be what we were taught we were supposed to be. We feel pressure to make it work, often to the detriment of ourselves. What we desire though, is to thrive.

Over the past twenty years, I've often thought that if I could just get one area of my life running smoothly, I'd feel okay, and the pressure would subside. I use the same approach with my house in that I feel okay if there's at least one space that I can be in and not see a list of things that need doing. In all those years though, I don't think I ever achieved even a day where I felt like I had my shit together at work, at home, with my kids or partner, with my health, or in any other way. There was always something weighing on me saying that I wasn't doing enough or being enough. I just wasn't enough.

That's not life. That's not thriving. That's a missed life; a wasted life. It's a race that's impossible to win and one that I no longer want to be in.

What I want is a gentle life where I feel like I'm thriving in whatever it is I'm doing. I don't want to cook for my family simply because I have to. The food would be rushed, not well made, and likely not very good. I want to take my time in the kitchen and lovingly create the foods my family loves and that will nourish them. I want to feel joy while baking that loaf of bread or those after-school cookies for my daughter. I want to thrive with passion, compassion, humor, and style.

Even in today's world where simple survival feels expensive, you are enough, and your life can be about thriving. Throughout this journey together, you've explored your Why and dreamed about the life you want; the one where you thrive. You've learned a little about the basics of personal finance and spent some time thinking about your relationship with money and how you've been using it. Those are big steps towards your goals and I'm proud of you.

So, what's next? How exactly do you get from where you are now to that life you dream of? Well, to be blunt, that's up to you. If you've followed the exercises laid out in the book, you should have a budget and an understanding of where your money is going as well as the changes you need to make. You know whether you need to make more money or educate yourself. You should understand if your feelings of fear or risk avoidance are holding you back. Where you are now will be unique to you so there is no simple path to follow.

To set yourself up for success, you need to start where you are and use what you have. There will be wins and losses along the way. You'll probably experience setbacks but also wins. You need to step forward, always. Each day, week, or month, think about one thing that you can do to move yourself toward your goals.

The best place to start is anywhere. Literally, doing anything towards your goal is a step in the right direction. Now, I am a big advocate for having a plan and executing it well, but I am also a busy mom who has learned the art of "do something." When I was exhausted with little children at home and an endlessly messy house, I used to just pick one thing I could get done without the expectation of doing any more. If once I finished that one thing, I decided to do another, great. If not, super. It wasn't about getting everything done or doing anything perfectly. It was about doing something and doing it "good enough." That way, I could feel a sense of accomplishment.

The most important thing to do is to do something, anything. But, if you're like me and you like a plan, I've outlined these six steps to help you develop your path.

Step 1 – Know your Why

We've already gone over this, and I probably sound like a broken record, but make sure you have a clear reason for this journey. Without it, the tough times will feel tougher.

Step 2 – Identify three small things you could do to help you get there

With that clearly defined Why, take all your thoughts, hopes, and dreams that have come up while reading the book and turn them into plans. Start by identifying three small steps you can take now, or soon that will get you closer to your goals.

Step 3 – Identify one big thing you could do to help you reach your goals

With the easier or more immediate steps out of the way, what's one big step that you can take toward your goals? This could be the thing that scares you or something that takes more time.

Whatever it is, write it down, then identify some of the smaller parts of that big thing.

If your big thing is education, you could look up potential courses or admission requirements. If you want to start investing, you could identify the accounts and assets that might work for you, and then learn more about them.

Step 4 – Decide on a timeline

For each of the steps you identified, determine a realistic timeline. Remember, flexibility is your friend so don't be too rigid, but also don't be so lax that you end up procrastinating.

Step 5 – Put your plan into action

A plan is just that. Don't let your dreams get lost because you failed to take the most important step. Using your list, decide on the one step you're going to complete and do it now. Right away. Then, when you finish that one, do the next one. Keep going until you run out of steps.

Step 6 – Revisit

As you complete tasks or if your circumstances change, which is more likely than not, you will likely need to revisit your plan. This is okay; adjust and add or remove steps to fit you.

Whenever you're stuck, and not sure what to do next, why not read a book? Books have helped me negotiate a better salary, move up the corporate ladder, take the plunge into investing, better my business, invest in real estate, and grow my confidence. Whenever I want to do something new, I learn about it. I was interested in real estate for years but didn't take the plunge until I had watched, read, or listened to experts and others who had done it first. It's how I learn and feel comfortable taking steps forward, even when things feel scary.

When I ran for public office, I listened to podcasts that featured women leaders, especially if the hosts or guests were or had been politicians. I also joined a weekly group taught by politicians and experts in their fields to learn about the ins and outs of campaigning. I made many friends through that group and coupled with my pre-existing network, had many conversations in the year leading up to the election about campaigning and serving. I even had the opportunity to practice campaigning with our Premier. All these learning opportunities were free.

I was once provided with a job offer that, while more than what I had been making, was priced low for my experience and the company I had applied to. At the time, I was reading a book about negotiation called *Never Split the Difference* by Chris Voss. Using the tips I learned in the book and some basic math, I was able to convince the hiring manager to increase their offer by more than 10%. All it took was a single email.

I believe completely in the power of learning through reading. It's why I'm writing this book. I have read hundreds of books and articles that have shaped my thinking in all aspects of my life. By writing this book, I am taking all that knowledge and paring it down into what worked for me. But, as I've said before, just because it worked for me, doesn't mean it will work for you.

I was on a business trip a few weeks before I left my corporate job. There were colleagues there from other offices around the country and some new acquaintances. During one of our team dinners, a colleague, whom I had known through minimal interaction for about a year, told me he was surprised to learn I was a business owner. "No offense" he started by saying, but he told me I just didn't seem the type. This was a person who had repeatedly underestimated me at work and who set me up multiple times to look like I had failed (the corporate world really is a nasty place). The thing is, this guy never saw my worth or my value because I wasn't necessary for his success. I'm underestimated a lot, and many people don't know my story. That's probably true for you too. I'm sure there are areas of your life or strengths that you have that others just don't know. If we don't show them, they'll never know.

What this guy didn't care to know or recognize was that I was a fierce competitor in this game of life. While he thought he was beating me and so much better, I'd already won. I could leave the corporate world behind and be okay. I could live my life while he was busy trying to climb the corporate ladder. He will eventually hit a ceiling while my potential is endless. I have this power and ability within me, as we all do. But by choosing to look at it, choosing to take it out and get to know that power; that is how you get to the life you imagine.

I've talked a lot in this book about stepping outside of your comfort zone and doing things that are big or scary. You may be asking how exactly to do that. "But Cherish, I don't even know where to start", you might be saying. Or "easy for you to say, you can write your book because you don't work, and your kids are mostly grown. You must not remember what it's like to have little kids and be constantly exhausted." Well, yeah. That's probably true. But while I don't work, I still run multiple busy businesses. I may not have little kids, but even with grown children, you never stop worrying about them or trying to support them. We all have our own lives to live with our own challenges and it's best to keep our eyes on our own paths so that we can make the best decisions for ourselves.

While reading this book, you may have felt overwhelmed at times thinking about how far you might be from financial freedom. That's okay. What I hope you take away is the knowledge that you can improve your financial well-being. You can take the next step, and the next, you can decide what matters to you and what doesn't, and you can look for opportunities to help you meet your goals.

You don't have to do everything at once. No one is expecting you to be a finance expert by next week. But you can take stock of where you are now and where you want to be. You can begin to chart a path to get there, even if you don't have all the answers yet. You can do one thing. And then the next thing. Before you know it, you'll be looking back to where you are now and be amazed at how far you've come.

You got this.

1. *A generational portrait of Canada's aging population from the 2021 Census*, Statistics Canada, April 27, 2022. https://www12.statcan.gc.ca/census-recensement/2021/as-sa/98-200-X/2021003/98-200-X2021003-eng.cfm.

2. Heisz, Andrew and Richards, Elizabeth. *Economic Well-being Across Generations of Young Canadians: Are Millennials Better or Worse Off?* Statistics Canada, April 18, 2019. https://www150.statcan.gc.ca/n1/pub/11-626-x/11-626-x2019006-eng.htm.

3. Canadian Millennials are drowning in debt, Financial Post, March 13, 2023. https://financialpost.com/moneywise/canadian-millennials-are-drowning-in-debt-four-tips-to-help#:~:text=Household%20debt%20hit%20%242%2C811%20billion,student%20loan%20debt%20as%20well.

4. Jezer-Morton, Kathryn, *Millennials in Canada*, The Canadian Encyclopedia, October 16, 2019. https://www.thecanadianencyclopedia.ca/en/article/millennials-in-canada

5. Evans, Pete. *Millennials earn more than their parents did – but owe a lot more*, CBC News, April 22, 2019. https://www.cbc.ca/news/business/millennials-income-statistics-canada-1.5106460.

6. Heisz and Richards, *Economic Well-being*

7. Heisz and Richards, *Economic Well-being*

JUST ONE MORE THING, BEFORE YOU GO

Thanks so much for reading. You've just taken the first step to investing in your financially free future. Way to go! If you enjoyed reading this book, I'd like to ask you to leave a review on either my website or Amazon. Reviews are a great way for you to support me as an author and they help other people just like you to find my book.

www.cherishwinsor.com/reviews

CONTINUE YOUR JOURNEY

As a special offer for getting this far in your financially free journey, I'd like to offer you a free 1-on-1 coaching session with me.

Visit my website to learn more: Cherishwinsor.com/coaching-offer

ACKNOWLEDGEMENTS

I have to start off by thanking my partner, Curtis. From the beginning of this process, he has been my biggest cheerleader, taking the time to read early drafts or offer words of encouragement and a glass of wine after a particularly difficult day of editing. He is my partner in everything and I'm grateful to have him by my side for this and every other adventure. Thank you, my love.

To my kids, who have heard me talk about this book for months, thank you for listening, even though it was probably really boring. Know that every time you asked about the book or gave me a quick hug while I sat at my computer, you were giving me the encouragement I needed to keep going.

They say raising a child takes a village and the same can be said about producing a book. Writing was the easy part and I'm so thankful to have had a team of folks to help get this book into the hands of readers. To Sarah, editor extraordinaire, thank you for your patience and willingness to answer every question, no matter how small. Your encouragement helped turn what seemed like a jumbled collection of words, into an actual book. Thank you to my early readers, Karli, Mercedes, Shelly, Kate, Tori, and Stephanie. Your helpful suggestions and eagle eyes were invaluable.

Finally, thank you to every mentor, manager, leader, and friend whom I have relied on for advice, support, guidance, and help. We are all lifelong learners, and my journey would not have been what it was without you.

Made in the USA
Monee, IL
04 November 2026

67383607R00075